# LORCA'S *POET IN NEW YORK*

## The Fall into Consciousness

*Betty Jean Craige*

THE UNIVERSITY PRESS OF KENTUCKY

ISBN: 0-8131-1349-0

Library of Congress Catalog Card Number: 76-024339

Copyright © 1977 by The University Press of Kentucky

A statewide cooperative scholarly publishing agency
serving Berea College, Centre College of Kentucky,
Eastern Kentucky University, The Filson Club,
Georgetown College, Kentucky Historical Society,
Kentucky State University, Morehead State University,
Murray State University, Northern Kentucky University,
Transylvania University, University of Kentucky,
University of Louisville, and Western Kentucky University.

*Editorial and Sales Offices:* Lexington, Kentucky 40506

To my mother and
in memory of my father

# Contents

# Acknowledgments

I would like to thank Professor Francisco García Lorca for his kind permission to quote sections of his brother's poetry as published in Lorca's *Obras completas* (Madrid: Aguilar, 1969). I would also like to express my appreciation to professors Frank Jones, Marcelino Peñuelas, and Michael Predmore for their reading of this study of *Poet in New York* in the course of its progress, and to Mrs. Sheila Bailey for her help in proofreading.

# Chapter One

# Introduction

In the early decades of the twentieth century Western Europe and the United States experienced an explosion of creativity in the art world: Picasso's *Les demoiselles d'Avignon* appeared in 1907; Stravinsky's *Rite of Spring* and Duchamp's *Nude Descending a Staircase*, in 1913; Joyce's *Ulysses* and Eliot's *The Waste Land*, in 1922; Kafka's *The Trial* and *The Castle*, in 1925 and 1926; and Faulkner's *The Sound and the Fury*, in 1929. The twenties saw the rage of surrealism, with the issue of Breton's *First Manifesto* in 1924 and the publication of the journal *La Révolution Surréaliste*. And in 1929 and 1930, while visiting Columbia University in New York City, the Spanish poet Federico García Lorca wrote *Poet in New York*.

*Poet in New York*, when finally published as one volume in 1940, was hailed as a product of Lorca's surrealist period, for it had been written after the poet's close relationship with Salvador Dalí and Luis Buñuel, who were both immersed in the movement.[1] Lorca himself had participated actively in the propagation of the ideas of surrealism in 1928 by founding and editing *Gallo*, an avant-garde magazine which acknowledged the influence of "Picasso, Gris, Ozenfant, Chirico, Joan Miró, Lipchitz, Brancusi, Arp, Le Corbusier, Reverdy, Tristan Tzara, Paul Eluard, Aragon, Robert Desnos, Jean Cocteau, Stravinsky, Maritain, Raynal, Zervos, André Breton, etc., etc."[2] In fact, Lorca had experimented with the new styles dominating the Spanish literary magazines in his prose-poems "Nadadora sumergida" ("Submerged swimmer") and "Suicidio en Alejandría" ("Suicide in Alexandría"), probably written in the summer of 1928 when he was in Cataluña with Dalí's family;[3] but, as he says in a letter to his friend Sebastián Gasch, "It is not surrealism, careful!, the clearest consciousness illuminates them."[4]

The New York poetry was indeed a startling departure from the poetry of Lorca's *Libro de poemas* and *Romancero gitano*, and because of its surface resemblance to some of Breton's and Eluard's surrealist poetry, *Poet in New York* was generally categorized as surrealist. Consequently it received only minor critical attention as a serious work of symbolic expression which was influenced by surrealism, certainly, but was finally illuminated by "the clearest consciousness." Yet when the poems are analyzed structurally (as well as imagistically and thematically), they reveal not a new technique of poetic creation adopted by the poet, but rather a sudden, radical estrangement of the poet from his universe. Lorca has gone from the state of participation in nature and in his community manifested in the rhythmical, frequently dramatic poetry of imagery drawn from the natural world of southern Spain (in *Romancero gitano*) to a state of extreme alienation now expressed in the dissonant subjective poetry of violent imagery drawn from the technological world of New York. Thus *Poet in New York* is the symbolization of Lorca's experience of depression and isolation in a foreign reality he apprehends as a hostile chaos. It is therefore the account of his psychic journey from alienation and disorientation toward reintegration into the natural world.

*Poet in New York*, however, transcends the poet's private vision of modern civilization: it becomes modern man's recognition of the spiritual "waste land" in which he discovers himself alone, empty, without roots, and without a god. Locked in the cell of his subjectivity, he no longer belongs to the world and no longer moves in time to the rhythms of the cosmos. For now he is "conscious," and his vision separates him from the world and his gods; now he is "fallen."

Modern man's retreat from the world into the recesses of self has transformed the world into the contents of his consciousness and made it real only insofar as it relates to his subjectivity. The harmony he once knew when he belonged to his community has been replaced by the anguish of separation he experiences when the community disintegrates and he finds himself alone in a world of relative values. Such radical reorientation in the universe has as its metaphor the Fall from the Garden of Eden, after which man wanders lost through the world aware of absence and isolation. Between the self and God, between the self and nature, between the mind and the body has opened an abyss not to be bridged by conscious man. The myth of the Fall expresses both the state of man's alienation from God and nature, resulting from consciousness, and the state of modern civilization's alienation from any spiritually unifying reality which might have held society together as a community.

*Poet in New York* is a vision of a fragmented world deserted by the gods; it is a vision of a dehumanized civilization whose sickness is born of consciousness and manifested in a material technocracy of empty suits of clothing. New York is a concrete symbol for a world in which "things fall apart; the centre cannot hold" (as Yeats wrote in 1919): there is no longer a center, a god or unifying myth, to serve as an absolute; and without such a center human life becomes a meaningless, monotonous, material existence of "imperfect anguish." The poet is assassinated by the sky (in the first line of the volume). The child has the blank white face of an egg. Automobiles are covered with teeth. The New York dawn groans. Money, in furious crowds, devours abandoned children. The moon becomes a horse's skull. The river gets drunk on oil. And "the metallic sound of suicide . . . revives us every morning."

In Lorca's New York there is no real death and no real life: "true pain or sorrow is not present in the spirit. It is not in the air nor in our life nor on these smoke-filled terraces"; there is only the "hueco"—emptiness, vacancy, the void—born of man's separation from nature and his gods. The tree, universal symbol of the axis of the world, with its roots holding fast to the earth and its branches reaching into the heavens, is now a "tree trunk that cannot sing," without roots and without branches. There is no connection. The ritual sacrifice by which primitive societies reaffirmed their ties to the earth and the heavens, thereby obtaining spiritual renewal, has long been forgotten; and this modern civilization needs such a symbolic death now to destroy the dehumanizing materialism that is draining it of life.

In his isolation within this world Lorca can at first only name the destructive forces which batter his subjectivity, invade him and deprive him of his identity, disorient him and cut him off from his roots in the earth; he can do no more than cry out in anguish against the incomprehensible universe. However, in the course of his stay in New York, after naming this strange world, the poet begins to understand the workings of the mechanical society that robs men of their humanity; and as he begins to recognize the forces of evil therein he gradually recovers his own identity and oneness with the force of the blood.

Such is his journey, from agonized impotence before a hostile chaos to outrage against the oppressive civilization that suffocates the poet and dams up the blood of human vitality. His quest is for renewed harmony with the natural world in which the blood (and his poetry, metaphorically identified with his blood) may flow in time with the cycles of the cosmos. With respect to the civilization of New York City, such renewed harmony is only possible after an apocalyptic revolution by which the dammed-up blood may be released in a symbolic societal self-sacrifice; with respect to the poet, such renewed harmony can only be achieved after the catharsis of his own symbolic ritual sacrifice which may reunite him with the universe from which he has been estranged. For the ritual sacrifice is the means whereby mankind may participate in the "periodical renewal of the World" (death and resurrection), may imitate the natural rhythms and momentarily know a wholeness once again. By the end of the volume the poet is approaching reconciliation with the natural world.

Federico García Lorca's expression of the twentieth-century reality he beholds in New York City is profoundly subjective, for the poetry is born of his private anguish of alienation. Yet it is by this profound subjectivism that *Poet in New York* is finally a universal, "objective" vision of modern civilization, for the poet whose cry issues from the primordial depths of experience is the voice of mankind—in this case modern man separated from nature and abandoned by his gods—giving words to the pain of his time. Thus the vision is somehow familiar to us, as are the visions of Eliot's *The Waste Land* and "The Hollow Men," of Yeats's "The Second Coming," and of Pound's "Hugh Selwyn Mauberley." These poets all see "a botched civilization," an "unreal city," a world where "the light is buried by chains and noises in the impudent threat of knowledge without roots." Rootless knowledge— this is the meaning of the fall into consciousness.

## Chapter Two

# Poet in New York and
# Lorca's Earlier Poetry

The song wants to be light.
In the dark the song has
threads of phosphorus and moon.
The light does not know what it wants.
In its limits of opal,
it encounters itself,
and returns.

(p. 361)

The tasting of the fruit of the Tree of Knowledge and the fall into consciousness put Adam and Eve outside the gates of the Garden to wander lost and alone, made ever restless by the memory of the Garden's harmony. It is this memory in man's now inescapable consciousness that impels the human search for a paradise, that brings the knowledge of absence and death, that finally makes possible the rare mystical union with God or with nature—the perishable bliss. As absence and death bring into being the poet, so the awareness of separation from God or nature brings into being Lorca's poetry, which contains throughout, implicit in its "tragic rhythm," the mystical yearning for peace. In his early poems Lorca presents the theme in such images as that of the ant who longs to touch the stars. In *Poet in New York* this yearning is mutilated by the city world; consequently the theme of life reaching beyond itself becomes that of life being cut off or suffocated, to be presented in such images as those of the poet without arms and the tree trunk which can no longer stretch upward toward the sky. But the longing to reach upward does not die when the poet's arms are severed. The impulse remains.

*Poet in New York* is a vision of modern civilization that Lorca has not had before, yet it is a vision issuing from the same emotional responses to the world that gave rise to *Libro de poemas, Poema del cante jondo, Canciones,* and *Romancero gitano.* The expression of Lorca's confrontation with New York City differs radically from the expression of his experience before he left Spain as a result of his new radical alienation from the universe and the accompanying loss of identity. But the deepest motivating forces within his personality do not change. Thus the themes which underlie the poems of these early volumes—the themes of the desire for the unattainable, the nostalgia for a lost Eden, and the sterility of self-consciousness—reappear in *Poet in New York* with not only personal but also social and metaphysical implications. An examination of some of Lorca's poems written before he went to New York may therefore help to make intelligible the surrealistic (but symbolic) New York poems.

Although Lorca's early poetry cannot be justifiably pronounced "mystic poetry," as the term is applied to the poetry of Saint John of the Cross, *Libro de poemas* and *Canciones* contain what may be described as a mystical desire for the unattainable, for peace, for the stars. "The song wants to be light" expresses Lorca's reason for being: the song (the "canto") reveals man's desire to be reunited with nature. For in the darkness in which the "canto" is born there are "threads of phosphorus and moon," sparks that want to be reunited with their center, the sun. The cold moon has no heat of its own and can only reflect the sun; but the sun, the "luz," is sufficient unto itself—perfect, round, whole, the wholeness which the poet remembers and desires (p. 211).[1] And the "canto" may be related to the "Duende," the "black sounds" that rise out of knowledge of death, of darkness, as the force of the blood, the force of life.

Lorca's early poem "Mar" ("Sea," p. 276), of *Libro de poemas,* is closely related to "The song wants to be light" and merits examination for its relation to some of the poems of *Poet in New York.* The first stanza contains its essence:

> The sea is
> the Lucifer of the blue.
> The heaven fallen
> for wanting to be the light.[2]

Lucifer was expelled from heaven for wanting to be God—which was the sin of pride, Adam's sin. So the poem may be read as a metaphor for the Fall, the separation from God which brings into being the song that "wants to be light." The blue sea condemned to eternal movement, suggesting the continual flux from which Lorca longs to be freed to rest in the stillness, reflects the perfect sky, as the fallen angel Lucifer remembers his lost home in heaven.[3] The sea can never be the sky, nor can it ever be still. But from the sea's bitterness at being rejected by heaven, from mankind's pain in separation from God, comes Venus, the goddess of love. Human love is born of Adam and Eve's desire to be reunited, to regain momentarily the feeling of completion and wholeness which they once knew in the Garden. Hence the beauty in the sadness, the beauty in the dark violence of the sea. Lucifer carried light (the memory of God) to the depths of the sea (the unconscious) to make the sea ever restless (conscious) in its longing for God; thus the sea's blue reflects the blue of the sky. And Lucifer is man (lines 27-28).

Implicit in Lorca's mystical impulse is the unrealizable goal; his tremendous passion is never to be satisfied. And implicit in the metaphor of the Fall is a nostalgia for lost innocence. Both these motifs in *Libro de poemas* reappear in *Poet in New York* with added social implications.

The theme of longing to see the stars is essentially mystical and tragic. It appears in many of Lorca's early children's poems, such as "Los encuentros de un caracol aventurero" ("The encounters of an adventuresome snail," p. 175), where an ant is condemned to death for having seen the stars. Of this poetic fable Edwin Honig comments, "The design of tragedy is already sketched . . . : hunger for the illimitable; a society whose moral laws are severe unto death; the suffering which comes of frustration; and the inevitable punishment meted out to the innocence of spirit."[4] And in Lorca's early play "El maleficio de la mariposa" ("The witchcraft of the butterfly," p. 669), a cockroach falls in love with a wounded butterfly who tells him of the beautiful world she sees; after she grows well and flies away, he is forever tormented by the longing to fly and forever unhappy dwelling in the dark earth.

Throughout *Libro de poemas* the "demand to embrace no less than the All" is apparent:[5]

> Lord, uproot me from the earth! Give me ears
> that may understand the waters!

Give me a voice that for love may uproot
their secret from the enchanted waves,
to light their sole beacon I ask for
oil of words.

(p.275)

Over the old landscape and the smoking hearth
I want to launch my cry,
sobbing from me as the worm
deplores its destiny.
Asking for what belongs to man, Love immense
and blue like the poplar trees of the river.
The blue of hearts and of force,
the blue of myself,
that may put into my hands the great key
that may break into the infinite.
Without terror and without fear before death,
frozen with love and with lyricism,
although the ray of light may wound me as it wounds the tree
and may leave me without leaves and without cry.

(p. 287)

This is the passion of Eros that brings pain to Lorca as a young man and throughout his life, the passion that is essentially tragic by the impossibility of its fulfillment.

Such intense desire for union necessarily implies separation, thereby suggesting the fall into consciousness, by which man cannot escape the awareness of his "self" as an entity separate from nature. The distance from nature wrought by man's intellect leads ultimately to sterility (in *Poet in New York* as well as in many other modern works of literature, such as *The Waste Land* and *The Sun Also Rises*) and to sleeplessness (in "Sleepless city," p. 492, and in "A Clean, Well-Lighted Place"); and sleeplessness is the inability to escape painful consciousness even for a moment. Thus sterility and sleeplessness have become symbols of the modern state of civilization and the modern psychological state of man.

Yet in *Canciones* Lorca expresses this same anguish—on a personal level—in the imagery of the natural world, an anguish which he will later generalize and express in the imagery of the urban technologized world of New York City. In "Canción del naranjo seco" ("Song of the barren orange tree," p. 420) he asks,

> Woodcutter.
> Cut from me my shadow.
> Free me from the torture
> of seeing myself without fruit.
>
> Why was I born among mirrors?

Lorca identifies himself with the tree, as he frequently does in *Libro de poemas* (and as he does indirectly in *Poet in New York*), for a tree has roots in the earth and branches that reach towards the sky. But the tree here is barren; it cannot bear fruit because it can see its own shadow. When the emotions—the vital energy—of the tree turn inward, the tree stands alone, sterile, unable to participate naturally in the cycle of life. Perhaps if it were not among mirrors, if it could not see itself, it would bear fruit; so it cries out, "I want to live without seeing myself."

Nostalgia belongs to self-consciousness as an inherent part of the awareness of the isolation of the self, for the knowledge of absence and separation contains within it a vague memory of a prior state of wholeness and, therefore, a desire for this state. In other words, the knowledge of absence postulates a lost presence. Very early in his poetry, while still in Andalucía, Lorca expresses a nostalgia for his lost childhood:

> My heart of silk
> has been filled with light,
> with lost bells,
> with lilies and bees,
> and I shall go far away,
> beyond those mountains,
> beyond those seas,
> near the stars,
> to ask Christ
> Our Lord to return to me
> my long-ago soul of a child,
> mature with legends,
> with the cap of feathers
> and the wooden saber.
>
> (p. 251)

The taste in his mouth that evokes the yearning for his lost child's spirit is "the taste of the bones of my great skull"—the taste of death.

The nostalgia for paradise, the pain of self-consciousness, the desire for the absolute, and the anguish of frustrated love form the thematic structure of almost all of Lorca's poetry and drama. Now let us turn our attention to the New York poems in which these basic themes are realized in imagery shockingly different from that of *Libro de poemas*.

*Poet in New York* is a poetry of anguish and outrage, a poetry of the solitary individual isolated within a chaotic, hostile universe with which he has no communication. The apparently surrealistic imagery expresses a very different world from the Andalucía of *Libro de poemas;* yet the poetry reveals an attitude toward the world that is not, finally, radically different from that of Lorca's early twenties. The poet who longed to touch the stars, elegized Juana la Loca, knew the taste of death within his bones, and yearned for his innocence forever gone is the same poet who raises his cry against the modern, dehumanized civilization of New York. But now the personal meaning of the myth of the fall into consciousness has become social, and consciousness has attained concrete reality on a societal level. The poet's voice becomes the cry of the blood against the myriad office buildings, the river drunk on oil, and the suits of clothing empty of humanity, all of which represent the results of the development of man's intellect. And in the midst of all the noise the poet's desire for a moment of stillness and fulfillment (not to be had) and his nostalgia for childhood grow ever stronger, as Eden grows more remote. So as Lorca formerly identified with the tree that could not bear fruit because of its self-consciousness and therefore could not participate fully in nature, by the end of *Poet in New York* he identifies with nature, with the blood and human vitality of natural violence, and fights the sterile "waste land" of the "sleepless city." He takes the side of the Negroes of Harlem and their great desperate king, for they still have red blood racing furiously through their veins, and they will rebel. In his anguish he experiences all the pain of consciousness, and, rendered passive by the impact of this metallic world upon his suffering sensibility, he can only name the objects of his nightmare vision. But in his outrage, when he has sufficient strength to react against this world, he calls for a revolution that will flood the streets with blood and destroy forever "all the friends of the apple and the sand" (p. 479), the bloodless suits of Wall Street.

Lorca's vision of the civilization of New York City is one of rootless consciousness by which man has separated himself from the creative forces of the earth and has lost his "sacred time and space" through loss of belief in any supernatural reality.[6] He is, as it were, without roots and without branches. In "Vuelta de paseo" ("Return from a walk," p. 488), the opening poem of *Poet in New York*, the image by which Lorca symbolizes man's dehumanized condition is a tree stump (suggesting a telephone pole), the "árbol de muñones que no canta," that does not sing. The tree, heretofore symbol of the "cosmos, and . . . its capacity for endless regeneration," is now cut off, dead, incapable of following the cycle of the seasons.[7] In Lorca's earlier poem "Manantial" ("Spring" or "Source of water," p. 272) the tree symbolized man's longing to reach beyond himself, for man is similarly pulled between the earth and the heavens, between matter and spirit. And in the poem "Este es el prólogo" ("This is the prologue," p. 582) he identifies himself as poet with the tree:

> The poet is a tree
> with fruits of sorrow
> and with withered leaves
> from crying for what he loves.
>
> The poet is the medium
> of Nature
> who explains her grandeur
> by means of words.

Thus it is clear that the truncated life represented by the tree stump in "Return from a walk" is the poet's own.

"Return from a walk" presents Lorca's initial experience with New York as a crisis of identity in which he becomes so disoriented in this world divorced from nature that he loses the sense of who he is. The poet who has been the "medium of Nature" has lost his reason for being; he has become uprooted from the very earth that gave him birth (as man and poet), and he is threatened by the sky to which he had formerly raised his arms and eyes. There can be no poem when the heavens, emptied of God, now suffocate man, rather than bring him spiritual life. For the poem, in its desire "to be light," springs from the earth as an arrow towards heaven, and without a heaven the poem has no reason for being. The tree trunk will not sing.

Assassinated by the sky,
between the forms that go towards the serpent
and the forms that seek the glass,
I shall let my hair grow.

With the tree stump that does not sing                                    5
and the child with the blank face of an egg.

With the small animals with broken heads
and the ragged water of dry feet.

With all that has deaf-mute weariness
and the butterfly drowned in the inkwell.                                 10

Bumping into my face that is different every day.
Assassinated by the sky!

It is significant that the first word of this book of poetry is "asesinado" ("assassinated"), a past participle modifying the poet. The poet is thus passive, a victim unable to act in the world; and without any god to inhabit the world and make life inherently meaningful, he is alone. The poem therefore consists of a series of images representing the unintelligible universe closing in upon the poet, whose only reaction against it is expressed in the phrase "I will let my hair grow." It is enough for the poet to name the chaos in which he has lost his identity, for he will not regain his identity and his original attitude towards external reality until he defines this world, or makes it recognizable.

The poet is "assassinated" between the forms that go towards the serpent and the forms that seek the crystal, between the subway and the glass roofs of the skyscrapers. The serpent retains here (as in *Poet in New York* as a whole) its meaning of the snake in Eden that gave Eve the apple and thus awoke her to consciousness. As an image of the subway the serpent also suggests a concrete labyrinth, a concrete Hades, in which man is completely cut off from the light of God.

Various images which seem unconnected in "Return from a walk" reflect the poet's crisis of identity and disorientation. The child with the blank white face of an egg may be compared to figures in some of De Chirico's paintings as an expression of mass-man, without identity, individual spirit, or meaning. No longer the symbol of innocence, wholeness, and hope, this child will grow up to be "hueco," empty. And the butterfly, which earlier was a symbol of the poet's heart

(p. 190) and spirit, is now drowned in the inkwell, another victim of the printed word, of the intellect.[8]

Jung has stated that the image of multiple faces and eyes implies psychic disintegration: the loss of wholeness and identity.[9] Lorca's image of "bumping into my face that is different every day" expresses such a disintegration of the self resulting from loss of contact with both the earth and the heavens. His loss of contact with God is his loss of contact with the self, and with the creative forces of his own unconscious and the collective unconscious. His symbolizing faculty is now overwhelmed by fragments of a world whose wholeness he cannot see and which appears itself to be disintegrating. No longer is he the voice of his people or of nature. Now he is the voice only of his isolated self, whose identity is uncertain.

In discussing metaphor, Cecil Day-Lewis has written:

It is surely not fanciful to suggest that the profusion of novel imagery we find in the metaphysicals, in the post-symbolists, and the poets of our own time, has its source in certain historical conditions; for, if the image is a method of disclosing the pattern beneath the phenomena, it seems reasonable to argue that, when a social pattern is changing, when the beliefs or structure of a society are in the process of disintegration, the poets should instinctively go farther and more boldly afield in a search for images which may reveal new patterns, some reintegration at work beneath the surface, or may merely compensate them for the incoherence of the outside world by a more insistent emphasis on order in the world of their imagination.[10]

The new universe Lorca apprehends in New York must first be named and somehow recognized before he may proceed to act appropriately within it. Earlier the words anguish and outrage were used to describe Lorca's reaction to his new situation, and these words express emotionally the essential rhythm of many of the poems (and of the volume as a whole) which may be abstracted as follows: first, the presentation of the image (the poet's vision of the world), and then a plea for action, a threat, etc. This rhythm represents the poet's turning from passive reception to action, and the language changes accordingly from a highly symbolic, illogical expression of vision to a more discursive, logical expression of action. Susanne Langer, in a discussion of Ernst Cassirer's *Philosophy of Symbolic Forms*, has written:

For in language we find two intellectual functions which it performs at all times, by virtue of its very nature: to fix the pre-eminent factors of experience as entities, by giving them *names*, and to abstract concepts of relationship, by talking *about* the named entities. The first process is essentially hypostatic; the second, abstractive. As soon as a name has directed us to a center of interest, there is a thing or a being (in primitive thinking these alternatives are not distinguished) *about* which the rest of the "specious present" arranges itself. But this arranging is itself reflected in language; for the second process, assertion, which formulates the *Gestalt* of the complex dominated by a named being, is essentially syntactical and the form which language thus impresses upon experience is discursive.[11]

Disoriented (psychologically, as well as physically and culturally) when he first arrives in New York, Lorca must "fix the pre-eminent factors of experience as entities, by giving them *names*," which he does in his poem "Return from a walk," a poem replete with nouns and relatively empty of transitive verbs. Indeed, as Del Río has pointed out, this volume of Lorca's poetry, more than any other, seems to be dominated by nouns, and a wide variety of them, which are rarely abstractions.[12] The images with which the poet orders his new experience in a society where his former values and beliefs no longer function are new in form, appropriate to the industrialized, bureaucratized civilization of that city. These new image forms he arranges to express a pattern representative of the new reality and his relation to it; and this pattern provides him with a recognizable context in which to act. Having named the objects of his vision, he may talk about them (in poems following "Return from a walk"), see relationships, and reaffirm his own identity and attitude toward this world. As the word makes order out of chaos by revealing and defining the world, so the word gives man power: the "Word discloses the daimonic, forces it out into the open where we can confront it directly."[13]

Lorca's New York poetry can be seen as a two-staged process in which he first defines his world by naming it (in surrealistic imagery of illogical language) and then reacts against it, imposing the demands upon reality which he has always imposed. The "pattern beneath the phenomena" which the poet discloses in his poetry comes from the poet's own mind. Consequently, we can speak of the fall into consciousness as the underlying myth not only of *Poet in New York*, but also perhaps of all of Lorca's poetry. For this myth is the symbolization in time of the knowledge of absence, which dominates the whole of his work.

Lorca's two poems of Section IV, "Poema doble del Lago Edem" ("Double poem of Lake Edem," p. 498) and "Cielo vivo" ("Living sky," p. 500), reflect in both form and theme the same "mystical" impulse that governs much of *Libro de poemas*: nostalgia for the state of innocence and desire for the beyond.

The very structure of "Double poem of Lake Edem" represents the split between man and nature—that is, man after the Fall—for the poem is a monologue of two voices of the poet: the first, a lyrical outpouring of the soul's pain and longing for lost childhood; the second (in the last stanza), an ironic self-glimpse which distances the former voice from the poet. Not to be heard here is a third voice, the "voice of long ago ignorant of the dense bitter juices," which the poet remembers and which evokes the feeling of the poem. This split within the self is consciousness.

It was my voice of long ago
ignorant of the dense bitter juices.
I divine it licking my feet
beneath the fragile wet ferns.

Oh long-ago voice of my love,                               5
oh voice of my truth,
oh voice of my open side,
when all the roses flowed from my tongue
and the turf did not know the impassible teeth of the horse!

You are here drinking my blood,                            10
drinking my humor of a naughty child,
while my eyes break in the wind
with the aluminum and the voices of the drunks.

Let me pass by the door
where Eve eats ants                                        15
and Adam fertilizes dazzling fish.
Let me pass the little men with the horns
to the forest of the stretching
and the happy leaps.

I know the most secret use                                               20
of the old oxidized pin
and I know the horror of open eyes
on the concrete surface of the plate.

But I don't want either world or dream, divine voice,
I want my freedom, my human love                                         25
in the most obscure corner of the breeze that nobody would want.
My human love!

The sea dogs pursue each other
and the wind awaits careless trunks.
Oh voice of long ago, burn with your tongue                              30
this voice of tin and talcum!

I want to cry because I have the desire,
as the children are crying on the last bench,
because I am not a man, nor a poet, nor a leaf,
but a wounded pulse that sounds the things of the other side.            35

I want to cry saying my name,
rose, child and hemlock on the banks of this lake,
to tell the truth of a man of blood
killing in myself the joke and the suggestion of the word.

No, no I do not ask, I desire,                                           40
voice of mine liberated that licks my hands.
In the labyrinth of screens is my nakedness that receives
the moon of punishment and the ash-covered clock.

Thus I spoke.
Thus I spoke when Saturn stopped the trains                              45
and fog and Dream and Death were seeking me.
They were seeking me
there where bellow the cows that have the hooves of a page
and there where floats my body between opposing equilibria.

The poem begins with the poet's hearing echoes of the innocent
voice of his childhood, echoes which elicit a passionate outcry for that
lost innocence whose voice was the voice of his truth. Perhaps (in line
5) the poet is equating "love" and the feeling of harmony with the
universe which he knew as a child, before "love" became an endless,
unsatisfiable longing. The apposition of the voice of his truth and the
"voice of my open side" metaphorically identifies the poet with Adam,

from whose side God took a rib to make Eve. When Adam is still in the Garden of Eden, inhabited also by God and Eve, he is not alone; his tongue speaks love: "all the roses flowed from my tongue."[14] The grass does not yet know the tooth of the horse, symbol of man's instinctual forces, for man is not yet at war with his instincts.[15] The "voice of long ago" is before lust, and before the "word" that distanced man from nature.

It is the voice of long ago that haunts the poet now, sucking his blood, as his acquired consciousness destroys the unity between his body (blood) and his soul, draining him of vitality. His eyes break with all that he sees; consequently he wants to pass through the gates of Eden to return to that first world.

The emotional impact of stanza 5 is one of horror derived from the mind's automatic and irrational joining of the pin and the eyes in an image only obliquely suggested by the discursive language of the verse in which the two objects are juxtaposed. Carlos Bousoño, in a study of "qualifying displacements," speaks of language as being essentially analytical; he suggests that the poet attempts to reproduce a "state of the soul" by using language in a nondiscursive way, illogically perhaps, so that he may communicate the "synthetic" nature of his feeling (which cannot be reduced to logical description) through the intuition, rather than the reason, of the reader.[16] This is what Lorca does in such a line as "Hay un dolor de huecos por el aire sin gente" ("There is a pain of hollows in the air without people," p. 472), where the intuition apprehends the image spatially as a "state of the soul," with an immediacy sometimes not present in the reception of more discursive speech. However, in lines 20 through 23, the poet is not synthesizing but rather analyzing (taking apart) an image for the reader; and the reader will synthesize the elements into the whole (not necessarily willingly) when he has the two images juxtaposed spatially in his mind.

Now the poet's voice grows cosmic (in stanza 8) as it rises from the primordial depths of his race to become the cry of all suffering men. As the "wounded pulse" of blood, the poet serves as the bridge between man and man, and between this present state of consciousness and the world of harmony on the other side; he temporarily becomes one with all humanity.

The climax reached here is sustained momentarily by the repetition of "I want to cry," and by reaffirmation of the poet's self, toward which the entire poem moves. He wants to cry out, now speaking his name, which contains "rose, child and hemlock"—the whole meaning of the poet's existence and of all of Lorca's poetry. For this is the tragic cycle of life, as the rose is love, both carnal and divine (as in Dante); the child is innocence, wholeness, and hope; and the hemlock is death. Such is the truth of the human race, before its destruction by the intellect. The "joke," which is made possible only by man's self-distancing (irony), and the "word" represent the post-Edenic cerebral world, the intellect's conquest of nature. In their position at the end of the line "blood" opposes "word," forming the social and metaphysical conflict which underlies all of *Poet in New York*.

In the final stanza, which serves as the denouement—the dying of the passionate intensity of the climax—there is a change of voice ("Thus I spoke"); and the conscious mind is now distanced from the irrational cry of pain. This change to an ironic voice accords with the pattern of the poem: the longing for harmony with nature (innocence), a passionate cry from the poet's depths in which he momentarily loses his individuality, and the fall back into isolated self-consciousness. Looking back intellectually to the spent emotions of the rest of the poem, the poet once again feels alone; and he becomes aware that death is approaching, seeking him between the "opposing equilibria."

"Cielo vivo" ("Living sky," p. 500) is appropriately placed as the second of the two poems of the section "Poems from Lake Edem Mills," for this one actually achieves the expression of a mystical moment, after the dark pain of the "Double poem of Lake Edem."

I shall not be able to complain
if I did not find what I was seeking.
Near the dry rocks and the empty insects
I shall not see the duel of the sun with the creatures of living flesh.

But I shall go to the first landscape                                    5
of shocks, liquids and murmurs
that penetrates a newborn child
and where all surface is avoided,
to know that what I seek will have its white center of bliss
when I fly midst love and sand.                                         10

There the white frost of the closed eyes does not reach
nor the lowing of the tree assassinated by the caterpillar.

There all the forms entwined maintain
a single frenetic expression of advance.

You cannot advance through the swarms of corollas          15
because the air dissolves your teeth of sugar,
nor can you caress the fleeting fern leaf
without feeling the definitive surprise of the ivory.

There beneath the roots and in the marrow of the air,
the truth of things mistaken is understood,                20
the swimmer of nickel that lies in wait for the finest wave
and the herd of nocturnal cows with the red feet of a woman.

I shall not be able to complain
if I did not find what I was seeking;
but I shall go to the first landscape of wetness and lashes          25
to know that what I seek will have its white center of bliss
when I fly midst love and sand.

I fly fresh as always over empty river beds,
over groups of breezes and boats run aground.
Reeling, I bump into fixed hard eternity                   30
and love to the end without dawn. Love. Visible love!

The title, which may also be translated as "Live sky" or "Living
heaven," suggests a spiritual world encompassing this one whose do-
main is not that of the dry rocks and empty insects (line 3). The object
of the poet's seeking is to be found in the "first landscape" of the
newborn child, where the poet may fly towards the white center of his
joy. Here "blanco" means both whiteness and the center of a target; in
the former sense it suggests the ecstatic moment of mystical union
(after the "dark night of the soul"), and in the latter sense it suggests
arrival at the goal of "what I seek." The image of flying is common to
mystical poetry as well; here it is a flight toward the whiteness of
perfect completion of longing, which in Neoplatonic terms would be
toward the One.

   Beneath the earth and in the marrow of the air the truth of life is
understood, on the other side of the urban world of *Poet in New York*
which is devoid of blood and spirit. In the seventh and final stanza the
poet switches from the subjunctive with which he has been expressing
his future flight toward his "white center of bliss" ("cuando yo *vuele*
mezclado con el amor y las arenas") into the indicative, bringing the

poem, and the flight, to a climax. The poem concludes in the poet's present ecstatic moment—ecstatic meaning out of the natural state. The poet is free of the natural cycle, free of dawn, for dawn indicates the new day and therefore the painful cycle of time and change, light and darkness, birth and death. At this mystical moment the poet is beyond the consciousness of time and into eternity.

Thus the rhythms of Lorca's earlier mystical poetry, in which the poet desires union with nature, recur in *Poet in New York* as a passionate longing for Eden: "Over the old landscape and the smoking hearth I want to launch my cry" becomes

> I want to cry saying my name,
> rose, child and hemlock on the banks of this lake,
> to tell the truth of a man of blood
> killing in myself the joke and the suggestion of the word.

This anguished desire comes to its climax in "Living sky," when the poet breaks through the bonds of the joke and the word to achieve a momentary fulfillment in the final ecstasy of "Amor. ¡Amor visible!"

Just as the rhythms of Lorca's early poetry continue to shape his New York poetry, so the Christian imagery of *Libro de poemas* continues to dominate the vision of *Poet in New York*. However, the Christian symbolism of the latter volume is frequently ironic, with the imagery representing finally the modern loss of spirituality, the failure of belief. In "Grito hacia Roma" ("Scream toward Rome," p. 520) Lorca employs Christian symbolism first to express a vision of a civilization destroyed from within by its own decadence and loss of sustaining religious myth (as Rome was destroyed) and then to invoke a prayer that the will of the Earth may be fulfilled. The symbol of Rome is ambiguous, for on the one hand, Rome was a decadent civilization, yet, on the other, it remains the papal seat, symbolically the center of the Church and also of human spirituality.

> Apples lightly wounded
> by the fine little swords of silver,
> clouds scraped by a hand of coral
> that carries on its back an almond of fire,
> fishes of arsenic like sharks,

5

sharks like tears to drown a multitude,
roses that wound
and needles installed in the tubes of the blood,
enemy worlds and loves covered with worms
will fall on you. They will fall upon the great dome          10
that the military tongues anoint with oil
where a man urinates on a dazzling dove
and spits crushed coal
surrounded by thousands of bells.

Because now there is no one to share the bread or the wine,          15
nor anyone to cultivate grasses in the mouth of the dead man,
nor anyone to open the linens of repose,
nor anyone to weep for the wounds of the elephants.
There is nothing more than a million blacksmiths
forging chains for the children that will come.          20
There is nothing more than a million carpenters
that make coffins without a cross.
There is nothing more than a crowd of laments
that open their clothes to await the bullet.
The man who deprecates the dove should speak,          25
should cry out naked amid the columns,
and give himself an injection to infect himself with leprosy
and let out a sobbing so terrible
that his rings and telephones of diamond may be dissolved.
But the man dressed in white          30
does not know the mystery of the wheat,
does not know the moan of childbirth,
does not know that Christ may still give water,
does not know that the coin burns the kiss of the prodigy
and sheds the blood of the lamb on the idiot beak of the pheasant.          35

The teachers show the children
a marvelous light that comes from the mountain;
but that which comes is a collection of sewers
wherein cry the dark nymphs of cholera.
The teachers point out with devotion the enormous improved
    domes;          40
but beneath the statues there is no love,
there is no love beneath the eyes of hard crystal.
Love is in the flesh torn open by thirst,
in the tiny hut that fights the flood;

love is in the ditches where the serpents of hunger fight,          45
in the sad sea that rocks the dead bodies of the sea gulls
and in the dark penetrating kiss beneath the pillows.
But the old man with translucent hands
will say: Love, love, love,
acclaimed by millions of dying ones;                               50
will say: love, love, love,
amid the quivering tissue of tenderness;
will say: peace, peace, peace,
amid the shiver of knives and melons of dynamite;
will say: love, love, love,                                        55
until his lips become silver.

Meanwhile, meanwhile, oh!, meanwhile,
the blacks that take out the spitoons,
the boys that tremble beneath the pale terror of the directors,
the women drowned in mineral oils,                                 60
the crowd of hammer, violin, or cloud,
will scream although their brains may blow out on the wall,
will scream in front of the domes
will scream maddened by fire,
will scream maddened by snow,                                      65
will scream with their heads full of excrement,
will scream like all the nights together,
will scream with a voice so torn
that the cities tremble like little girls
and the cities of oil and music break,                            70
because we want our daily bread,
flower of the alder and threshed tenderness,
because we want to be fulfilled the will of the Earth
that gives its fruits for all.

The poem opens with the word "Manzanas" ("Apples"), announcing
the theme of the Fall, which here represents the separation of the
society from any spiritual reality. The apple is pierced by small silver
swords, as the wholeness of man's original state has been pierced by his
intellect, the symbolism of which is suggested by Lorca's frequent
association (in *Poet in New York*) of the intellect with the function of
cutting.[17]

From lines 3 through 10, as in the earlier poem "Muerte" ("Death,"
p. 506), there is a series of subtle "becomings," indicating a world of

continual (and painful) change. The clouds are scraped by a coral hand in a violent image of tearing (as the heavens are torn open by sky-scrapers), and the coral hand has on its back "an almond of fire," thus metamorphosing into the image of poisonous fish and then into the image of sharks. So what is happening to the fish, the traditional symbol for Christ? The sharks metamorphose into "tears of sobbing to blind a multitude"; and the rose (love) now brings pain.[18] The image of needles installed in the tubes of the blood, in the veins of life, is a shocking suggestion of violent penetration. Furthermore, the word "caños" has overtones of metal and machinery, as it usually means pipes, conduits, etc.; so the human body is being given the characteristics of the technological world. The image of needles is followed by an image of death and decay: "loves covered with worms." The images, surrealistic in their effect, are piled up one upon another until they represent a tremendous emotional weight that falls in upon Rome, for Rome symbolizes both Western civilization and the Church. The poet names the elements of his vision, and then he prophesies the collapse of the civilization. All of this will fall in upon the great dome of Saint Peter's, which the military tongues now anoint with oil used to make war. In line 12 appears the image of a man urinating on a dazzling "paloma" ("pigeon" or "dove"), symbol of the Holy Ghost, and spitting out crushed carbon as thousands of church bells ring out; such to him is the meaning of the great dome and the dove of the Holy Ghost.

In a secular world the Mystery of the Mass is forgotten. Lorca recognizes the religious meaning of bread in his early poem "Canción oriental" ("Eastern song," p. 257), in which he says, "La espiga es el pan. Es Cristo en vida y muerte cuajado" ("Wheat is bread. It is Christ in life and death materialized"). But now in New York there is nobody to break and share the bread and wine; there is no Body and Blood of Christ, for there is no one to recognize a spiritual reality beyond the material world. All will fall in upon Rome because there is no unifying myth to hold the civilization together in community. The loss of a fixed point in time and space—the focus of the Mass—means chaos and the relativity of values, with the inevitable consequence of alienation, for man is suddenly thrown back upon himself as the sole referent for his values. There is no center of the world by which man may orient himself, no given meaning to his own existence by which he may know his purpose for living; life becomes hopelessly material, meaningless, and monotonous.

Now there is nothing more than a million blacksmiths forging chains for the children about to be born, for no freedom exists in a material world, no release from its profane reality, because nobody performs the Mystery of Holy Communion in a world that does not know "Incarnation." The carpenters are making coffins without crosses, appropriate for the burial of a spiritually empty society.[19] Now "a crowd of laments" open their clothes to await the bullet; for with no spiritual release from this secular existence, time becomes a meaningless repetition leading only to decay and death.

The mandate from the poet appears in lines 25 through 29: the man who scorns the dove should cry out from among the columns (suggestive of Roman ruins as well as of New York City skyscrapers); he should inflict himself with the horrible biblical disease of leprosy and emit a howling sob that may dissolve his rings and telephones of diamond. But the man dressed in white (an ironic image, in that white is traditionally a symbol of purity and holiness, but here is meant to signify wealth and leisure) does not know the mystery of the wheat. He does not know how it grows, for he is totally alienated from nature; nor does he know what it symbolizes, for he is alienated from any spiritual reality. Nor does he know the moan of childbirth, by which the newborn child is brought to life through pain, naturally. And he does not know that Christ may still bless the waters and give spiritual meaning to human life.

The teachers teach the children about a marvelous light that comes from the mountain, but the only thing that comes is a sewer filled with the nymphs of cholera. In 1918, Lorca wrote,

> What is holy baptism,
> but God become water
> that anoints our foreheads
> with His blood of grace?
> For something Jesus Christ
> confirmed Himself in it.
> (p. 193)

However, in New York the water has become a carrier of disease and death, rather than of hope and renewed life; now there is no baptism. The waters grow stagnant, murky, covered with oil.

The devotion of the teachers is directed to the new, "improved" domes; but love is not to be found in the modern statues, whose glass eyes give them the appearance of mannequins, nor in this dehumanized, despiritualized world. Love is found instead in the poor flesh of poverty-stricken hungry people living in hovels and in the sad sea that rocks the bodies of sea gulls. It is the old man with translucent hands who will keep saying, "Love, love, love, peace, peace, peace. . . ."

Finally comes the apocalyptic vision that is both the climax of the poem (lines 57-70) and a threat to the civilization of white suits that step on the blacks who take out the spitoons. The downtrodden will begin to scream at the top of their lungs, and there will be no stopping them. They will scream until the cities tremble like little girls and until they break the prisons of oil and music,

> because we want our daily bread,
> flower of the alder and threshed tenderness,
> because we want to be fulfilled the will of the Earth
> that gives its fruits for all.

Thus the poem ends, after the climax of the "grito hacia Roma," with the calmness of a prayer that recalls the opening line of the Lord's Prayer; hopeless as the situation may be that brought it into being, a prayer necessarily contains hope. The final line is in the indicative: the Earth gives its fruit for all.

Now the social significance of line 15 can be noted: the rich will not share the bread and wine with the poor, and for that reason revolution must come. Perhaps the cry to Rome is not only a cry of anguish, frustration, anger, and bitterness, but also a plea for Rome to come to the aid of the poor, to awaken to what is happening in New York, to help bring Christ back into the world.

The structure of the poem follows the same general pattern discussed earlier of first giving names and then seeing relationships. In lines 1 through 9 the poet presents his perception of the world (in a symbolic form, by the very nature of language) in a series of images that build up to an almost intolerable weight before their release by the word "caerán" ("will fall"). The poet names the world and then prophesies its collapse. The repetition of "caerán" makes impossible any escape from the coming disaster.

Repetition (Whitmanian in tone) is used throughout the poem for building tension to a minor climax and then releasing that tension only to begin again in another direction toward another minor climax. Stanza 1 presents the vision and the prophecy. Stanza 2 presents the situation in negatives that imply the positive desired situation. Stanza 3 describes the situation in grammatically positive terms, with the repetition building up tension. And, finally, stanza 4 reaches the climax, the screaming point, after which the four concluding lines bring the poem and the passion to rest in a prayer that approaches intonation in its rhythm and meaning.

The illogical surrealistic images of the initial vision fade away, and the language becomes that of the simple people who want their daily bread; it is discursive, prosaic, "temporal" in form. When the poet understands relationships between the objects of his vision, then he can speak about the world in logical language, in "temporal form" (in a tone approaching the medium of music). It is the natural cycle of the Earth that is desired: a relationship in which man may live in harmony with the cosmos, sink his roots into the soil, and lift his arms toward the heavens. And as Lorca turns toward this relationship, his language simplifies and his tone changes. He becomes the voice of the people. The natural world of order is, and must be, expressed in simple language, without irony. The poem thus ends in hope.

I have referred to the "temporal form" of Lorca's early poetry as opposed to the "spatial form" of *Poet in New York*. The use of the terms "temporal" and "spatial" for literary form was established by Joseph Frank on the basis of the work of Wilhelm Worringer, who had observed that (in Frank's words), "When Naturalism is the reigning art style . . . we find that it is created by cultures which have achieved an equilibrium with the natural environment of which they are part. . . . On the other hand, when the relationship between man and the universe is one of disharmony and disequilibrium, we find that non-naturalistic, abstract styles are always produced. . . ."[20] According to Frank, art that is apparently three-dimensional accentuates the time value of the objects presented, connecting them with the real world in which events take place in time. And the perception of such art—a naturalistic painting, for example—takes place in time as well, for the eye must move back and forth in the picture to grasp the relationship of the objects to each other. However, nonnaturalistic art

eliminates time value in presenting the various components of the painting on a single plane, so that perception of them is simultaneous, as in
Pound's definition of the "image"—"that which presents an intellectual
and emotional complex in an instant of time." Frank discusses such
works as *Ulysses* and *The Waste Land* as examples of the "spatial form"
in literature towards which modern art is moving (in 1945). To grasp
the meaning of such literature the reader must apprehend the work as a
whole, in space, as he would apprehend a painting which cannot be
comprehended in time (that is, as the work unfolds in time).

   The poems of *Poet in New York* are not structurally similar to *The
Waste Land*, which itself functions as an "image." But the conception
(and subsequent perception) of the various images of Lorca's New York
poetry may be described as "spatial." As the expression of logical
relationships (of cause and effect—a temporal concept) within images
and between images implies an understanding of an ordered universe, so
the suppression of logical connection implies an apprehension of a
chaotic universe, incomprehensible to man. The enumeration of things
of different classes, as occurs in "Return from a walk," is therefore the
expression of a chaos which the poet cannot order.

   Let us first examine the "spatiality" of imagery in *Poet in New York*
and then look at the "spatial form" of some of the New York poems
(as opposed to the "temporal form" of the poems in the *Romancero
gitano*, for example). In "Return from a walk" appears the image of the
"ragged water of the dry feet" which is not logically representative of
any object in "external reality" (that is, the reality that men can
perceive in common) and which is not logically conceivable, given the
standard meanings of the adjective "ragged" and the noun "water." So
these two words represent two distinct concepts which must be apprehended simultaneously on a single plane by the mind, so that their
import may be somehow felt, if not understood, by the intuition.
However illogical this image—or double image, if "ragged water" and
"dry feet" are considered separately—may be in time (in discursive
reasoning), the image is not completely meaningless if apprehended
spatially, through the intuition and not through the reason. For the
adjective "ragged" will be drawn to "feet" in the generation of an
image which reproduces the poet's feeling. It is such displacement of
the adjective that Bousoño calls "desplazamiento calificativo," a
synthesizing process by which the poet attempts to communicate a

"state of the soul" that cannot be fully expressed in discursive, analytical language. Logical syntax is thus broken up (in a manner somewhat analogous to the process of analytical cubism in painting), and the language is rendered incoherent, so that the reader must reconstruct the image, or "state of the soul." Image formation, then, takes place largely within the mind of the reader. And images are perceived immediately, in space, not in time.

A similar process occurs in the perception of the poem as a whole, when the poem consists of a series of images or phrases whose interrelationship is not explicit. Various concepts must be held in suspension, on a single plane, by the perceiving mind. The poet who is naming the chaos cannot (yet) understand the relationships of the myriad things that bombard his mind; so he expresses no cause-and-effect relationships. The tree stump that does not sing, the hollows, the crowd of laments are all equally present, equally palpable, and equally real to the poet. By naming the chaos the poet is ultimately "forming new wholes" (in Eliot's words) in a synthesizing process whose result is a world finally familiar to the poet. At last the poet sees the pattern and calls for revolution.

The "spatial form" of *Poet in New York* reveals that the poet's initial reaction to the New York City reality is not a synthetic one by which he might identify foreign objects and see immediately their interrelationships, but rather an analytic one, by which he penetrates that reality and disintegrates it into apparently unrelated fragments. This reaction occurs in many of the poems throughout the volume, but it is most obvious in the first poem, "Return from a walk," where the poet apprehends the world as isolated elements, which may synecdochically or metaphorically represent larger realities, but which nonetheless appear here as unrelated images. This apprehension is, in fact, the function of consciousness, which sees separations, for it has pulled man away from God, so that God (or nature) becomes an object of its perception. And by making the self an object of its perception as well, consciousness creates an internal split by which man himself is no longer whole but fragmented.

The vision of a man living in relative harmony with the universe will be more or less synthetic, for the world will appear more or less orderly, and he will have appropriate myths to unite the parts into a comprehensible whole. In a harmonious relationship man sees connections between things; he sees the world metaphorically, in a few symbols, as in Lorca's earlier poetry, for the various parts of the universe reflect each other or are similar to each other. The vision of a man completely alienated from nature, however, will probably be analytic, for the world will appear not as an orderly whole but rather as a threatening chaos; and he will apprehend it accordingly, as fragments with no unifying relationship. Indeed his consciousness has destroyed the unity. The proliferation of images corresponds to the relativity of meanings in a state of spiritual anarchy, where there is no unifying myth by which all things might be identified with some ultimate reality. There can be few communally shared symbols in a world of relative values.

"Subjectivity is truth, subjectivity is reality" (Kierkegaard). If the only reality we can know is that reality apprehended through our individual subjectivity, then the radically increased isolation and self-consciousness which Lorca experiences will necessarily result in a peculiarly subjective vision of reality. The less self-conscious, less depressed, less isolated writer can narrate action which takes place outside himself (as Lorca was able to do in the *Romancero gitano*) and see order in the world that seemingly exists independent of his subjective perception of it. But the highly self-conscious, depressed, isolated poet can only tell of the world as it affects him, as it imprints itself upon his consciousness; he therefore cannot perceive what order it may have external to his existence.

*Poet in New York*, then, presents a static situation, whereas the *Romancero gitano* presents a dynamic situation; the latter is dominated by verbs expressing action. In the *Romancero gitano* Lorca narrates, from a third person point of view, action occurring in the world—in myth or history or his own imagination—which does not necessarily affect him. The tale unfolds in time as the poet tells it; so the tale imitates action temporally as that action might have taken place in actuality; it imitates the rhythm of time. Furthermore, these poems approach the medium of music in the rhythm of the verse, whose incantatory quality lowers the level of consciousness in the reader to participation in the action on a less than conscious level. The rhythm, in reducing consciousness, thus brings about a kind of merging between the reader and the world of the poems; for rhythm in words imitates the rhythm of the cosmos, suggesting a harmonious relationship between the individual (either the poet or the reader) and the cosmos.

In *Poet in New York* a revolution seems to have occurred in the poet's relation to "external reality." The incantatory rhythm of the *Romancero gitano* is gone, although it returns in the last poem of the volume, "Son de negros en Cuba" ("Sound of blacks in Cuba," p. 530), written after Lorca had left New York City and gone to Cuba. In its place is a verse of irregular rhythm and rhyme whose sound is frequently harsh. By the very dissonance of the New York poetry the reader is kept at a distance from the world described and is not seduced into participating vicariously in the action of the poet's world by a lowered level of consciousness. The reader remains fully conscious, shocked by the poet's images, and therefore as fully alienated from that hostile reality as the poet. Just as the poet is frustrated in his attempt to make order out of that chaos, so is the reader, who receives the unconnected, dissimilar images in the same way that the poet has perceived the chaos. With the disappearance of rhythm and discursive language, which would express logical relationships in time, temporal depth disappears. The reader now apprehends the whole series of images on the same flat plane and faces them uncomprehendingly.

Nor can the reader retain the illusion that he is a disinterested observer of the world presented in this poetry. Since the poet is no longer narrating action outside himself, but rather is expressing the impact of the world upon his consciousness, his poetry will necessarily be in first person or from the first person point of view. The reader then identifies with the voice of the poetry and perceives the world through the poet's eyes. Instead of imitating the rhythms of nature, the reader imitates the alienation of the poet from nature.

*Poet in New York*, then, does represent a revolution in Lorca's relationship with the natural world. The mystical longing for a moment of harmony with the universe which brings into being his early poetry is indirectly the motivating force of his New York poetry, as the theme of the Fall, ever present on a personal level in *Libro de poemas*, becomes the social and metaphysical theme of *Poet in New York*, where the word threatens the blood with extinction. And Lorca, in his initial confrontation with the city, experiences loss of identity and impotence against the universe from which he is radically alienated; he can only name the elements of his vision. The form of his poetry becomes "spatial." But finally he does recover his identity. As Lorca finds his voice, as he prophesies the collapse of the cerebral world which has made human beings bloodless, his poetry becomes more discursive, simpler. For when he knows again that he belongs with the forces of nature, then his verse reflects this recovered balance and unfolds in time, "because we want to be fulfilled the will of the Earth/ that gives its fruits for all."

*Chapter Three*

# The Fall into Consciousness

When Adam and Eve had eaten of the Tree of Knowledge of good and evil they saw that they were naked and they were ashamed. So they covered themselves with fig leaves. Thus were they separated from nature, from God, and hurled into the isolation of self-consciousness. Now they are "as gods, knowing good and evil." This act is the fall into consciousness by which man gains awareness of himself and loses harmony with nature. Man's vision turns the world, self, and God into objects of perception, and his subjectivity engulfs the universe. By recognizing no god, no absolute, existing outside his consciousness, man becomes his own god: good and evil become relative to himself. Finally he is alone, a stranger "in a universe suddenly divested of illusions and lights."[1]

As Adam and Eve wander across the face of the earth with the memory of Eden become a hope for Paradise, so man is condemned to seek forever the lost bliss. The split between the self and the world, the mind and the body, makes harmony impossible, while making the longing for completion inescapable. Consciousness is born of separation, and separation is born of consciousness; thus consciousness contains the archetypal knowledge of that wholeness which becomes the object of man's Faustian search. Hence the human impulse to transcend subjectivity and to reach such wholeness.

The desire to transcend subjectivity is essentially mystical when expressed as union with the divine or as union with nature, a "spirit that rolls through all things," the One, etc. For most men, however, this drive for completion is expressed as sexual desire: man transcends himself in union with the opposite sex, attaining a moment's ecstasy or loss of self in the achievement of this wholeness. The third possible lover, besides god and the mate, is death, by which man breaks out of the isolation of his consciousness through the annihilation of the self.

Between Eden and Paradise, between the remembered harmony and the moment of ecstatic union, between innocence and death, lies the ache of longing, absence, emptiness, the void—what Federico García Lorca calls the "hueco," the hollow—brought into being by man's fall into consciousness. The emptiness lies within the self, in the abyss opened between the mind and the body; and the emptiness lies within the world, in the abyss opened between the self and the universe. Man's consciousness has destroyed the myths and banished the gods, so that man finds himself alone under a vacant sky.

Federico García Lorca's *Poet in New York* is a vision of a civilization that has killed God by its extreme consciousness and now exists without roots, without sacred time and space, without hope for the morrow. Modern man has severed with his penetrating intellect the ties that once bound him to the soil, to his community, and to his god, and he ends up homeless. The community disintegrates and existence becomes purposeless.

The myth of the fall into consciousness underlies *Poet in New York* both thematically and structurally. Many of the poems fall into the rhythm pattern of vision (separation), desire for union or for apocalyptic destruction, the climax of such desire, and then rest. Furthermore, the volume as a whole has such a rhythm: vision, apocalypse, and reconciliation. Let us examine Lorca's "Nocturno del hueco" ("Nocturne of the void," p. 507) of the fourth section of *Poet in New York*, "Introducción a la muerte: Poemas de soledad en Vermont" ("Introduction to death: Poems of solitude in Vermont") as a poem fairly representative of the entire work in theme, language, and structure. Governed by the myth of the Fall, which expresses the essential dualism between the ego and the world, "Nocturne of the void" is an anguished cry issuing from the consciousness of the isolated poet whose yearning for wholeness is passionate and extreme and apparently not to be fulfilled.

I

*In order to see that all has gone,*
*in order to see the hollow ones and the dressed ones,*
*give me your glove of moon,*
*your other glove lost in the grass,*
*my love!*          5

The wind can pull out the snails
dead on the lung of the elephant
and blow the stiff worms
from the buds of light or the apples.

The impassive faces row                                                   10
beneath the diminutive cry of the grasses
and in the corner is the little chest of the frog
disturbed in his heart and mandolin.

In the great deserted plaza
was bellowing the recently severed cow's head,                            15
and of hard definitive glass
were the forms that were seeking the turn of the serpent.

*In order to see that all has gone*
*give me your hollow world, my love!*
*nostalgia of the academy and sad sky.*                                   20
*In order to see that all has gone!*

Inside of you, my love, through your flesh,
what silence of trains with-mouth-facing-upwards!
how much arm of mummy that has flowered!
what sky without exit, love, what a sky!                                  25

It is the stone in the water and it is the voice in the breeze
overgrowths of love that escape from its bleeding trunk.
It is enough to touch the pulse of our present love
in order that flowers may come up on the other children.

*In order to see that all has gone.*                                      30
*In order to see the hollows of the clouds and rivers.*
*Give me your hands of laurel, love.*
*In order to see that all has gone!*

The pure hollows are turning, in me, in you, in the dawn
conserving the tracks of the branches of blood                           35
and some tranquil profile of plaster that draws
instant pain of the punctured moon.

Look at the concrete forms that seek their emptiness.
Mistaken dogs and bitten apples.
Look at the anxiety, the anguish of a sad fossil world                    40
that does not find the accent of its first sob.

When I seek in the bed murmurs of the thread
you have come, my love, to cover my roof.
The hollow of an ant can fill the air,
but you go moaning without direction through my eyes.                    45

No, not through my eyes, that now you show me
four rivers pressed tightly in your arm,
in the crude shack where the imprisoned moon
devours a sailor in front of the children.

*In order to see that all has gone,*                                        50
*stubborn love, fled love!*
*No, do not give me your hollowness,*
*for now mine goes through the air!*
*Oh pity you, pity me, pity the breeze!*
*In order to see that all has gone.*                                        55

A line-by-line analysis of "Nocturne of the void" is probably the best approach to discussion of its particular theme and the book's general theme, which is both social and metaphysical. The title suggests the darkness of night; the poem is, therefore, a cry from the night, from the "void." It is man's separation from nature that allows man to see or think about what is not there; and it is his consciousness that allows him to conceive of a void or a vacancy—the absence of something that was once there and is now gone or of something that should be there: the God that walked in the Garden. Thus this is a poem about absence.

The opening line, to be repeated three times as part of the refrain, sets the tone: "In order to see that all has gone." Its tense evokes the past, implying the all that once was there. For the poet is speaking to his "amor mío" ("my love"), who, as the object of his love, is absent. The term is ambiguous, as it may apply to a person, meaning "my beloved," or to abstract love, meaning either the poet's abstract desired love object or his act of loving, without an object. In the latter case the "amor mío" would be an expression for his endless yearning for completeness, which remains unsatisfied because there is no love object or no hope for completion on earth. Another possibility related to this notion is that the poet is creating an abstract giant of love who contains the act of loving and the beloved object. Lines 3 and 4 (as well as the rest of the poem) bear out this hypothesis, that Lorca has invented a mythical figure, a personification of love whose gloves touch both the moon and the earth and who is therefore a mythical giant of nature.

This "amor mío" holds on to the moon, a traditional symbol of femininity which also symbolizes death throughout Lorca's poetry; and it holds on to the earth, which is also feminine, since the earth produces after being fertilized by rain from the sky, and which also suggests death, as it covers dead bodies. All of this is forecast in the title to the section: "Introduction to death."

In line 2 the words "los huecos y los vestidos" (which may be translated as "the hollow ones and the dressed ones," although "hueco" also means "void" or "vacancy," and "vestidos" means "dresses" or "clothes" perhaps with nothing inside) recall the earlier poem "1910," in which appear the following lines:

> There is a pain of emptinesses in the air without people
> and in my eyes creatures dressed without nude body underneath!
> (p. 472)

Adam and Eve naked in the Garden belonged to nature; but by the Fall they separated themselves from nature and became isolated in subjective perceptions of the world. In the course of the centuries, as the powers of man's consciousness increased to build eventually a world of machines, man's mind lost relation to his body; he became alienated from nature and from himself: "suits of clothing without nude body underneath." What Adam and Eve put on to hide their shame from God—the fig leaves—became suits of clothing that no longer contained nature, but were empty, "hueco." So Lorca's image of bodiless suits of clothing presents not only the extreme of the alienated consciousness, but also the extreme of the human being who has lost even the memory of Eden and hence lacks the spirituality that defines the suffering self-consciousness of Lorca and impels the endless search for wholeness. The "huecos" and the "vestidos" have gone beyond the pain of consciousness to the point of being unaware of their loss.

The poet (in lines 3 and 4) seeks union with his "amor mío," whose gloves touch the moon and the grass, and so he is asking for a mythical expansion of himself which will eventually lead him to the vision that "all has gone." Such union with this "amor mío" as may bring wholeness and completeness to the poet, then, means being taken into nature by death.

The second stanza (lines 6 through 9) is surrealistic in its language and imagery. Yet there is a poetic or thematic logic running through the entire poem that suggests the images are symbolic in origin. Both snails and worms feed on bacteria and the remains of living animals; and the small, disgusting creatures of the earth often, in *Poet in New York*, seem to be taking over a world abandoned by human life. Here the wind, generally a symbol of the spirit and a symbol of sexuality in Lorca's early "Preciosa y el aire" (p. 426), may blow away these dead snails and stiff worms that have feasted on animal life, the young green sprouts, and the apple. In the third stanza the oxymoron of impassive faces rowing (as would an oar on water) presents the image (one of suffocation) of unmoving faces beneath the earth—in graves on which grasses grow. It is the disturbed voice of the frog, primitive animal life, that is heard.

The "deserted plaza" of line 14 is a concrete representation of the "hueco." For the plaza is the center of the town, of traditional community life, and its desertion suggests the metaphysical notion that "the centre cannot hold." In this disintegration of the community human beings no longer have each other in that imperfect solidarity once possible. And the sound that breaks the awful silence is the bellowing of the recently severed cow's head. The cow, says Cirlot, is usually associated with the earth and the moon, as well as with motherhood; and by its lack of consciousness it may symbolize the pure life force in its functions of giving birth and giving milk.[2] Here the force of nature has been cut by modern civilization, whose knife-sharp intellect is capable of decapitating the cow. The Jungian psychoanalyst Jolande Jacobi has written, "The sword or spear often symbolizes the penetrating, 'cutting' function of the intellect," an observation that may illuminate much of the imagery of the New York poems, where not only cows but also sailors, trees, and the moon feel the destructive power of the cutting blade.[3] And the severed cow's head recalls the "tree stump that does not sing" of "Return from a walk" (p. 471).

Lines 16 and 17 are almost identical to line 2 of "Return from a walk": the "forms" seeking the turn of the serpent may refer to the subway. However, the frequent use of imagery from the Garden of Eden throughout *Poet in New York* lends symbolic weight to this particular image, for the serpent tempted Eve and thereby brought about the fall into self-consciousness; the serpent represents the material world which opposes God's heaven. On the level of social criticism, then, these "forms" may appropriately be associated with the subway. The image also suggests an underworld labyrinth: Hades or death.

Line 22, "Inside of you, my love, through your flesh," presents an image of sexual penetration that apparently here renders the "amor mío" as the poet's love object. Nevertheless, the association between his love (whether it be his beloved or a mythical giant of the concept of love) and death is present, for inside is the "silence of trains with-mouth-facing-upwards," with the flowered arm of a mummy (recalling lines 10 and 11) and a sky without exit. These claustrophobic images are more suggestive of death than of life. Similar images of suffocation (or drowning) recur throughout the New York poems, beginning with the line "Assassinated by the sky." In both images of the sky, heaven seems absent and the sky brings death.

The stone in the water and the voice in the breeze (of lines 26 and 27) suggest, respectively, the poet's soul and the poet's voice, which escape the "bleeding trunk" to speak. They are "bordes de amor," with "bordes" meaning the wild, uncultivated fringes at the edge of a civilized or ordered area, and they escape the bleeding trunk (a sexual image) of love. Or, if we see "amor mío" as death, then the poet's voice comes from the fringes of death, which he has known and will embrace. To touch the pulse in a normal love union would mean the conception and birth of children, but here (in lines 28 and 29) to touch that "amor" is enough for flowers to be born over other children (an image of grasses or flowers growing over faces of children buried in the earth that has appeared before). And the child, says Jung, is a symbol of wholeness and therefore of hope for the future.[4] Here the future of humanity is dead.

Again comes the refrain but with a slight variation: now the poet asks, "Give me your hands of laurel, love," in place of "give me your hollow world, my love," of line 19, and "give me your glove of moon," of line 3. The hands of laurel tie the "amor mío," which gives the poet his sense of incompleteness by being a "mundo hueco" (line 19), to man's consciousness, for the laurel as a symbol of knowledge is associated with the sun god Apollo, who, as Rupert Allen has pointed out, is "Lord of man's consciousness which has emerged from the depths of the oceanic unconscious."[5] Thus if the "amor" gives the poet the "hands of laurel," then he will be able to see that all has gone; his seeing, in fact, brings into being his longing for his "amor mío" to bring

an end to his incompleteness, an end that would be death. The reference to laurel points to the Daphne-Apollo myth as one of particular
importance to Lorca, for he had called himself a "Dafne varonil"
("male Daphne") in an early poem (p. 272) in which he merges with a
poplar tree. (Perhaps his identification with Daphne and consequently
with the tree suggests a desire to escape physical love and become an
unconscious part of nature.)

In stanza 9 dawn contains, or brings to consciousness once again, the
void; it does not bring hope for the new day because in New York,
when dawn arrives, "nobody receives it in his mouth" (in the poem
"Dawn," p. 497). The blood imagery of line 35 is reminiscent of the
earlier violent sexual penetration, as is the image of the "luna apunti-
llada" ("punctured moon" or "moon brought to a point," of line 37),
symbol of femininity and death. Perhaps the moon too has been
stabbed by the sword of the penetrating intellect (which has created the
"hueco"). Perhaps the intellect has taken even from death her natural
function in the universe. (In "Ode to the king of Harlem," p. 479, the
moon is made of asbestos.) The concrete forms of a civilization emptied
of spirit seek their own voids.

Now even the dogs have lost their instinct and are without direction
because of the bitten apple; for consciousness led to the overdeveloped
intellect and eventually to the atrophy of natural powers and instincts.
The poet, however, is apart from the dehumanized fossil world which
"does not find the accent of its first sob," for he still retains a vague
memory of Eden that is the source of his anguish and his knowledge of
the void. He still retains the essence of humanity, condemned to
consciousness, whereas these spiritually petrified "hollow men" (to use
Eliot's term) have somehow gone beyond the state of suffering awareness. It is the echo of that first sob that moves the poet to want to
embrace his "amor mío" and gives him the desire for wholeness, for
death and reabsorption into nature.

In lines 42 through 45 the poet senses the approach of his "amor
mío," and his language becomes more gentle: "you have come, my
love, to cover my roof." He feels secure in the shelter of his beloved;
and he is almost overcome by the presence. This stanza and the
following suggest again that the "amor mío" is a fictional giant, cosmic
lover, the image of love-death personified. It may also be an image of
the center of the world, for it contains an allusion to the Garden of

Eden in the image of the "four rivers pressed tightly in your arm"; as told in Genesis 2:10, at the foot of the Tree in the Garden four rivers flow.

In lines 48 and 49 the moon figure, imprisoned in the hut, devours the sailor, who travels on the seas, as Christ walked on the water. (There are several sailors who meet death in the New York poetry: in "Christmas on the Hudson" the sailor has his throat cut, is "degollado," beheaded. And the word "devora," of line 49, relates to the image of drowning in several other poems.) The death occurs in front of the children: they see its absurdity and will thereby come to consciousness themselves. The moon (the feminine principle) brings death.

Man is helpless in the face of this "stubborn love, fled love," this cosmic love-death reality that stands firm; that is, man cannot rid himself of the longing to go outside himself to gain completeness. But the poet cannot have his "amor mío"—it is an "amor huido" ("fled love"), and the union is not to be realized now. The poet's longing has no object: hence his pain, the "hueco." The "amor mío," the presence of death, leaves him alone in his agonizing consciousness. All is gone now, even the possibility of escape in death.

Part I of "Nocturne of the void," then, concludes with the plea, "No, do not give me your hollowness ("hueco"), for mine now goes through the air!" And the poet is left locked in his own subjectivity. Part II centers completely on "Yo" ("I"). "Yo," on a line of its own, begins five of the seven stanzas of the section; and "Yo" represents the passive self-consciousness that can only record the violence of the unintelligible world bombarding it. Here, except for the two italicized stanzas which serve as a refrain, there are no active verbs: the poet is simply naming his visions.

II

I.
With the whitest void of a horse,
mane of ash. Plaza pure and doubled.

I.
My void penetrated with its armpits broken.                    5
Dry skin of neuter grape and asbestos of dawn.

*All the light of the world fits into an eye.*
*The cock crows and its song lasts longer than its wings.*

I.
With the whitest void of a horse.                                              10
Surrounded by spectators who have ants in their words.

   In the amphitheater of the cold without mutilated profile.
Through the broken capitals of the bloodless cheeks.

   I.
My void without you, city, without your dead men that eat.      15
Equestrian definitively anchored by my life.

   I.
*There is no new century or recent light.*
*Only a blue horse and a dawn.*

The image of a white horse with an ash-colored mane is presented in
the first stanza by virtue of its logical denial: "the very white void of a
horse," an image reminiscent of the white horse of Revelation 6:2. An
omen of death throughout much of Europe, the white horse suggests
the ghost of a horse, and in *Poet in New York* it may suggest the death
of the primal instincts of the unconscious. White traditionally symbolizes purity, chastity, the absence of sexuality, while also meaning pain
or sorrow to Lorca.[6]

The "Plaza pure and doubled" is not thematically distant from its
immediately preceding image, for this geometrical form, devoid of the
human content which brought it into existence, calls up again a feeling
of emptiness: the plaza stands abandoned and Godforsaken (as in line
14 of Part I). In fact, the deserted plaza is central to Lorca's vision of
New York City, in which the isolated individuals are no longer held
together spiritually by any unifying myth.

In line 5 the word "hueco" appears again, as it does in each line of
Part II that follows a line of "Yo"; that is, stanza 1 begins "Yo./Mi
hueco sin ti. . . ." Thus "Yo" contains the "hueco." The fifth line
presents the sharp juxtaposition of the irrational abstract image of the
"hueco" with the naturalistic image of "broken armpits"—a shocking
corporeal equivalent of "hueco," perhaps.

In the following line the dry grape skin supports imagistically the
theme of the loss of natural vitality, for grapes and wine symbolize the
life forces by their mythological association with Dionysus and the
power of the spirit by their religious association with the sacrificial
blood of Christ. This relation to the Last Supper is reinforced by the

allusion in line 8 to the rooster which crowed upon the denial of Christ; here the rooster's crow also suggests the end of night, the ending of the nocturne. All the light of the world fits within the eye; the poet sees all; his consciousness penetrates the world.

Line 11 presents a paranoiac image: the poet is surrounded and threatened by spectators with ants in their mouths, ants that can consume a man. (The ants appeared in Part I, line 44.) His being the center (as "Yo" is the center of this section) expresses increasing passivity since the first section of the poem in which he could at least look out to the violent world; here he is conscious only of his "Yo."

There is an almost Dalí-esque metamorphosis of the cold, hard broken capitals of the amphitheater into bloodless cheeks, a juxtaposition of images which presents again the parallel of a decaying civilization and a decaying, dehumanized people, empty of color, life, and blood. Paradoxically, the word "desangrada" calls into being the very thing that it denies, becoming in this way a violent image itself; as a past participle it implies a deterioration of a state: the cheeks once had blood in them. The broken capitals echo the broken armpits of line 5 and thus semantically unite the human body with the deteriorating amphitheater.

The poet withdraws his "hueco" (the emptiness of longing within which has come to define his being) from the threatening, inhuman world, from the "dead men that eat," that, like the empty suits of clothing, no longer retain any humanity; neither alive nor dead, they represent the destructive force of death that feeds on vitality.

Line 16 recalls the horse imagery, but again the image is put forward only to be negated. "Equestrian definitively anchored by my life" is an image of paralysis: the poet's life is anchored to the land, to consciousness, and he cannot move with the horse, the primal forces. If Part I of "Nocturne of the void" represents the poet's yearning to be united with his "amor mío" (perhaps death), a yearning that is ultimately frustrated, as he says at the end "fled love!," then this image of his being anchored to life and to his conscious vision is a thematic repetition of the final stanza of the first section, but with a resignation absent earlier in the poem.

There is no hope: "There is no new century or recent light." All that remains is the contents of the spent past and the poet's devastating knowledge—and the "hueco," his agonizing desire for completion or for an end to consciousness. The poem draws to a conclusion with the dawn. But this dawn has been clouded with asbestos (line 6) and thus is empty of its usual symbolic meaning of hope. On the other hand, a kind of equilibrium is reestablished after the violent, nightmarish outbursts of Part I. Part II is calmer; the poet has become passive, collapsed into his "Yo." The nocturne is over. When the cock crows, the night's tale comes to an end.

"Nocturne of the void" falls into the climactic rhythm that Kenneth Burke says embodies "the principle of the crescendo," for the poem consists of an increase of emotion to an explosion and then a recession of emotion.[7] This rhythm, which governs most of Lorca's New York poems, may also be described as a movement from vision to action, as in the following scheme: first, the presentation of the image, the representation of the world in the poet's subjectivity; then, a climactic supplication, plea for action, or threat, as typified by the phrase "It is necessary"; and finally a calm, or a diminishing of emotion.

Many poems in *Poet in New York* have this structural arrangement. "Ode to the king of Harlem" is composed of four parts and has several climaxes: "It is necessary to kill . . ."; "One must flee . . ."; "Then . . . you will be able to kiss. . . ." "Dance of death" leads up to "That the Pope may not dance!" The poem "Landscape of the vomiting multitude" commands "vomit! There is no other recourse." Its companion "Landscape of the urinating multitude" builds up to "It will be necessary to go. . . ." The most prophetic of such climaxes occurs in "Sleepless city," which warns, "Beware! . . . One day horses will live in the taverns . . . Another day we shall see the resurrection of the dissected butterflies . . ."; and then issues a call to action: "one must carry them to the wall where iguanas and serpents wait. . . ." "Moon and panorama of the insects" increases in tension to the line "It is necessary to walk. . . ." The Whitmanian "New York" culminates in "I denounce . . . and offer myself to be eaten. . . ." And "Scream towards Rome" builds to the repetition of the threat "will scream . . ." and then moves to prayer: "because we want to be fulfilled the will of the Earth that gives its fruits for all."

Almost every poem of the volume becomes the expression of some violent upheaval which is either personal or societal. It is as if Lorca first passively received the world into his consciousness, during which time he could only name the elements of his vision, and then summoned up his forces to react against the world, to act or to call for action. In the first part the images reflect the poet's alienation, and they are accordingly illogical, surrealistic, incomprehensible. In the second part, however, after the poet has identified the world, the language reflects his reorientation and his new understanding of his place in the world; consequently the language is more discursive, logical, and intelligible.

To see the world is to be separated from the world, to be alienated; to act in the world is to move with the world, theoretically in harmony with the rhythms of the universe. Therefore, the rhythm of vision to action is structurally the journey from separation to union. "Nocturne of the void" is central to Lorca's vision of New York City as his most anguished expression of separation; yet within the poem we can see that the pain of separation reaches a climax which represents a kind of union, a release from separation and from consciousness.

Mankind's separation from God represented by Adam's Fall is climaxed by the Crucifixion, whereby mankind is redeemed. Structurally, the story is similar to the Flood, the prophesied Apocalypse, the springtime ritual sacrifice of the god in primitive cultures, Persephone's four months in the underworld, and even the mystic's "dark night of the soul." In all of these, separation from the world leads to a climactic, symbolic death from which the world obtains new life.

The poet's quest in both "Nocturne of the void" and *Poet in New York* is for union, and it is Adam's quest. Throughout the New York poems the poet implicitly represents the fallen Adam isolated within his subjectivity. Lorca's alienation from the New York City world leads to solipsism and despair, until his consciousness, which gave birth to the emptiness, finally becomes the cutting edge by which he achieves his own symbolic death. Hence the images of the dead poet (p. 475), the armless poet sinking beneath the waves (p. 488), the beheaded poet spilling blood across the suburbs (p. 492), the poet losing his face (p. 514), the poet offering himself to be eaten (p. 517), etc. Through such symbolic self-sacrifice the poet moves from identification with Adam to identification with Christ, as the slain god by whom the earth is made new and harmony is attained.

The story of Adam and Eve's Fall and banishment from Eden symbolizes the human knowledge of absence, which is a momentary perception. To say that the poet of *Poet in New York* goes from being a symbol of Adam to being a symbol of Christ is not necessarily to say that in the earlier poems he is Adam and in the later poems he is Christ. The experience of separation, climax (symbolic self-destruction or symbolic destruction of society), and calm is expressed again and again within the poems themselves, each of which presents a climactic moment of vision. And this climactic moment of vision—actually a spatial perception—can only be expressed, or communicated, in time, as in a myth. Here that myth is the Fall, which generates the sacrifice.

*Poet in New York* reflects the influence of surrealism in both its use of language and its imagery. In "Nocturne of the void," for example, the illogical concept of union with the hollowness is communicated by the impossible image of the concrete, whirling "huecos"; and such expression is surrealistic. Yet there is a basic difference between André Breton's surrealist poetry and Lorca's symbolic poetry that inheres in the poem's conception. In the first *Manifesto of Surrealism* Breton defines surrealism, as he says, "once and for all":

Surrealism, *n.* Psychic automatism in its pure state, by which one proposes to express—verbally, by means of the written word, or in any other manner—the actual functioning of thought. Dictated by thought, in the absence of any control exercised by reason, exempt from any aesthetic or moral concern.[8]

Poetic creation "in the absence of any control exercised by reason" becomes radically altered from being a vehicle for the expression of ideas or emotions existing in the poet's mind to being a vehicle for a series of images not necessarily dependent upon an a priori subject: one image generates another.

Lorca's New York poetry functions symbolically, metaphorically. The irrational, illogical, surrealistic (but not surrealist) images together compose an organic whole expressive of a feeling or idea (not necessarily rational) in the poet's mind; and the images come into being by their relation to this a priori subject, rather than by their relation to each other. In other words, chance, which is at the root of surrealist creation, is not an active force in Lorca's volume. *Poet in New York* is therefore not actually surrealist poetry.

On the surface, however, Lorca's New York poetry and Breton's surrealist poetry both participate in the same wide-ranging cultural phenomenon of the movement toward spatial form: the poetry seems to move away from the medium of music and toward the medium of painting, as the image comes to dominate the expression. Joseph Frank, in his "Spatial Form in Modern Literature," asserts that twentieth-century literature in general expresses alienation from the natural world by moving away from a form that imitates the temporal rhythms of the universe and toward spatial form, by which objects are apprehended simultaneously on a flat plane in the form of an image. Both Frank and Ortega y Gasset discuss the turning away from the humanized art of the last century which reproduced the appearance of external reality and imitated the rhythms of the universe—in painting and literature as well as in romantic music that recreated human passions. The new art, according to Ortega, is dehumanized, and, according to Frank, has spatial form; that is, it is to be perceived as an image.[9] This change in form indicates man's suddenly increased alienation.

The juxtaposition of abstract and concrete nouns, by which abstractions become concrete, represents the apprehension of reality on a single plane, in which temporal depth disappears. Indeed, the illogical juxtaposition of unlike nouns—or unlike realities—presents an image which must be apprehended intuitively and immediately, in spatial form. For the two (or more) parts of the surrealistic image cannot be integrated or merged into one, but must be perceived simultaneously in all their separateness by the imagination, which holds them in balance as an irrational, irreducible image, as a painting. In the immediacy effected by this technique there is an opaqueness, or flatness, to the vision presented because of the absence of natural relationships between the components of the image, which will seem therefore to exist out of time. This kind of poetry is thus a movement away from the faithful reproduction of nature and toward a "derealization" (in Ortega's terms) of reality in which both the surrealists and the Lorca of *Poet in New York* participate. Lorca's New York poetry, which lacks the musical (natural) rhythm of his early verse, becomes more visual, closer to the medium of painting, as he becomes more isolated in his consciousness, further separated from nature.

# Chapter Four

# *Poet in New York:* The Vision

It is the blood that comes, that will come
over the sheds and rooftops, everywhere,
to burn the chlorophyll of the blond women,
to groan at the foot of the beds before the insomnia of the washbowls
and burst in a low yellow dawn of tobacco.

(p. 480)

"Ritual," says Northrop Frye, "seems to be something of a voluntary effort . . . to recapture a lost rapport with the natural cycle."[1] And it is ritual that has somehow been eliminated from the New York world Lorca sees which no longer even puts forth the "effort . . . to recapture a lost rapport with the natural cycle," to imitate the natural rhythms of the universe. As human vitality has vanished, so have real anguish, pain, and death disappeared from this unnatural world of "hollow men." What is needed is a violent cataclysmic upheaval by which this civilization may confront the forces of life, destroy the cancer within, and begin again: death and resurrection. The cancer of materialism is eating away the vitality of the now dehumanized society of New York City, and it must be burned out before these people may once again know the forces of the blood and the moon, the wholeness of a community.

The movement from prophetic vision to action, from "spatial form" to "temporal form" both within individual poems and through the volume as a whole, reflects a movement from the "epiphanic moment, the flash of instantaneous comprehension with no direct reference to time," toward ritual.[2] The action the poet calls for (after his vision) is a purgation—a symbolic death—necessary to the accomplishment of a reestablished order and harmony with the cosmos; for the universe must expel the evil within in order to survive. In this cycle of tragedy the hero recognizes the necessity of death and fulfills his destiny, so that order may be reestablished.

At the heart of the tragic vision is the myth of the descent—into night, winter, dissolution, death.[3] *Poet in New York*, in its demonic imagery as well as in its tragic rhythm, may be seen as an enactment of the myth of the descent by which the destiny of the disintegrating community is violently fulfilled in a dramatic purgation of the evil forces of chaos that have threatened the poet with his own extinction.[4] The myth of the descent into hell corresponds symbolically to the myth of the Fall, with the latter being a metaphor for the state of modern civilization which the poet sees here, and the former being a metaphor for the means by which this civilization may actively participate in its own destruction and effect its own salvation. In Christian terms, the "fortunate fall" leads eventually to the necessary sacrifice of a god by which all mankind may be saved. Without the ritual sacrifice, there is no salvation.

The self-destructive cataclysmic upheaval which society must undergo for its salvation is made necessary by malignant forces at work within society that are silently bringing about the death of humanity. Responsible for these forces is the developed intellect, the extreme consciousness of modern man that has "killed God," and severed man's bond to the natural world. For Lorca, the intellect has become a cutting edge, and he has been "degollado" ("beheaded"). "Navidad en el Hudson" ("Christmas on the Hudson," p. 491) is an expression of the poet's anguished helplessness in the face of this power which (in this poem) he cannot fight.

```
      That gray sponge!
That sailor recently beheaded.
That big river.
That breeze of dark limits.
That edge, love, that edge.                                          5
The four sailors were fighting with the world,
with the world of angles that all eyes see,
with the world that cannot be traveled without horses.
There were one, a hundred, a thousand sailors,
fighting with the world of high velocities,                          10
without knowing that the world
was alone in the sky.

      The world alone in the lonely sky.
It is the hills of hammers and the triumph of the thick grass.
It is the very live anthills and the coins in the mud.               15
```

The world alone in the lonely sky
and the wind at the exits of all the villages.

   The earthworm was singing the terror of the wheel
and the beheaded sailor
was singing the water bear that was to crush him;          20
and all were singing alleluia,
alleluia. Deserted sky.
It is all the same, the same!, alleluia.

   I have passed the night on the platforms of the suburbs
leaving my blood on the stucco of the projects,          25
helping the sailors to gather in their torn sails.
And I am with my hands empty in the sound of the mouth of the
     river.
It does not matter that every minute
a newborn child moves his little branches of veins,
or that the birth of the viper, unwinding beneath the branches,   30
calms the thirst for blood of those who see the nude.
What matters is this: vacancy. World alone. Emptying.
No dawn. Inert fable.
Only this: Emptying.
Oh my gray sponge!          35
Oh my recently severed throat!
Oh my big river!
Oh breeze of mine with limits that are not mine!
Oh cutting edge of my love, oh wounding edge!

    The poem centers upon the recently beheaded sailor in line 2 who becomes the poet in line 36, when the poet cries out, "Oh my own recently severed throat!" The sailor who sails the seas—the source of life, the unconscious—recalls the Christ who walked upon the seas, the fisherman who redeemed man. But the sailor has had his throat slit and can no longer speak: the poet is dead, having lost his voice. Consciousness is thus symbolized by the cutting blade that severs the ties man originally had with nature.

    The word "filo" ("edge") in line 5 means the cutting edge of the knife, and it is this "filo" that has decapitated the poet. But in line 39, the knife is love ("filo de mi amor"—"cutting edge of my love"), which suggests that, in line 5, "filo" is in apposition to "amor." The poem then becomes an agonized cry not only against the modern world of edges and angles (line 7), but also, as in "Nocturne of the void," against love which—unreciprocated—has cleft the poet in two. Metaphorically, the wound of love serves as the pain of consciousness, of separation. The alienated poet transfers his own emptiness and isolation to the surrounding world that is "alone in the lonely sky," circling meaninglessly in the universe now empty of God. It is a world in which one cannot live without horses (line 8)—without the life force, sexual energy—but instead of horses there are metallic edges and angles and high velocities.

The language of geometry that dominates the first stanza cedes its place to a language of the primordial world of vegetation in the second and third stanzas: thick grass, live anthills, mud, earthworms. The dense grass (that covers graves) triumphs where man finally does not; the anthills thrive, the mud sucks up the coins of civilization. Thus there is an air of emptiness, of an abandoned world (lines 16-17), and the worm sings of the terror of the wheel, which eventually dehumanized the planet. Rollers have flattened the earth for the construction of buildings and changed natural forms to edges and angles.

"And all sang alleluia" to an empty sky, for, unlike the sky at Easter to which this line is an ironic allusion, this "cielo" is vacant, abandoned by God. But, "it is all the same." Christ too was a sailor, a "marinero." Is there an identification being established here between the decapitated sailor sinking beneath the waves, an image recalling the armless poet sinking beneath other waves in the preceding "Landscape of the vomiting multitude" (p. 488), and the Christ who fails to rise into heaven? The title of the poem would recall the birth of Christ, who came to redeem man from the original sin of consciousness. This sin led to the wheel, to hammers, to geometry, to the whole technological civilization of New York. But where is Christ in this Christmas poem?

With the fourth stanza, the poem moves into first person singular. In lines 24 through 25, the poet says that he has left a trail of blood across the suburbs, across man's technological plans for constructing a mechanical future. Thus the poet becomes a Christ, shedding his blood in order to cleanse mankind of the effects of his consciousness. The shedding of his blood helps the other sailors to recover their sails torn by the sharp edges of the mechanical world. And the poet himself becomes the sacrificial lamb.

Every minute that a child is born, the snake moves. This is the snake of the Garden of Eden that brings man lust and separation from God. The innocent child is born into corruption, and when the child begins to try out his life, to move his "little branches of veins," the snake unwinds beneath the branches of the Tree of Knowledge. There is no escape. Once conscious, man is forever with thirst that takes the form of "the thirst of blood of those who look at nakedness."

What matters is the "hueco," the hollowness of the world alone in the sky. When man became conscious in the Garden of Eden, he was left forever incomplete, with a longing to experience wholeness once more. The world is alone, a "mundo solo," because it has been separated from God. The river of life empties into the sea.

There is no dawn (line 33)—no hope. Dawn is an inert fable or fiction that will no longer bring hope to man. In line 36 the poet identifies himself with the beheaded sailor; and the narrative description of the "mundo solo" in the first part of the poem becomes a lyrical outpouring from the poet's own soul. The great river (line 37) becomes the poet's own cry, his own life pouring forth into the sea (from his severed throat). The river is both blood and poetry, symbolically identified with each other throughout Lorca's poetry.[5] Consciousness, which in effect makes possible painful unreciprocated love and thus becomes identified with love, is that sharp edge that has cut the poet's throat and made him bleed into the sea.

The symbolic self-sacrifice of the poet in "Christmas on the Hudson" (which is metaphysical, as well as personal and private, in its implications) parallels the self-sacrifice of the society in its fallen state in "Oda al rey de Harlem" ("Ode to the king of Harlem," p. 478). The blood that is the poet's in "Christmas on the Hudson" is society's in "Ode to the king of Harlem," and it too will flow over the roofs of the houses in the suburbs. But in this latter poem the shedding of blood will effect a salvation, for it is, symbolically, the ritual sacrifice needed for the redemption of the world. Accordingly, the poem is ordered in a climactic arrangement in which the flood of blood climaxes the increasing tension of an oppressed people. By the end of the poem, after the prophecy that the Negroes will finally dance, there is a subsiding of emotion and a reestablished calm.

With a spoon
he was digging out the eyes of the crocodiles

and hitting the rumps of the monkeys.
With a spoon.

The fire of always was sleeping in the flint                          5
and the scarabs drunk from anise
were forgetting the moss of the villages.

That old man covered with mushrooms
was going to the place where the black men were crying
while the spoon of the king was crackling                             10
and the tanks of polluted water were arriving.

The roses were fleeing on the edges
of the last curves of the air,
and in the mountains of saffron
the children were crushing small squirrels                            15
with the flush of a soiled frenzy.

It is necessary to cross the bridges
and arrive at the black flush
in order that the perfume of the lung
strike our temples in its dress                                       20
of hot pineapple.

It is necessary to kill the blond whiskey seller,
all the friends of the apple and the sand,
and it is necessary to hit with closed fists
the little jewesses who tremble full of bubbles,                      25
so that the king of Harlem may sing with his people,
so that the crocodiles may sleep in long lines
beneath the asbestos of the moon,
and so that nobody may doubt the infinite beauty
of the feather dusters, the graters, the copper pots and the
          casseroles of the kitchens.                                 30

Oh Harlem! Oh Harlem! Oh Harlem!
There is no anguish comparable to your oppressed eyes,
to your blood shuddering within the dark eclipse,
to your garnet violence deaf and mute in the shade,
to your great king prisoner in a janitor's suit.                      35

The night had a crack and quiet salamanders of ivory.
The American girls were carrying children and coins in their
          wombs,
and the boys were fainting on the stretching cross.

It is they.
They are the ones who drink whiskey of silver next to the
    volcanoes                                                                    40
and swallow little pieces of heart, on the frozen mountains of
    the bear.

    That night the king of Harlem,
with a very hard spoon
was digging out the eyes of the crocodiles
and hitting the rumps of the monkeys.                                         45
With a spoon.
The blacks were crying confused
between umbrellas and suns of gold,
the mulattoes were pulling rubber bands, eager to arrive at the
    white torso,
and the wind was dirtying mirrors                                             50
and rupturing the veins of the dancers.

    Blacks, Blacks, Blacks, Blacks.

    Blood has no doors in your night facing upwards.
There is no blush. Blood furious beneath the skin,
alive in the spine of the dagger and in the breast of the landscapes,   55
beneath the pincers and bushes of the celestial moon of cancer.

    Blood that seeks along a thousand roads powdered deaths and
    ashes of nard,
skies rigid on a slant, where colonies of planets
may roll along the beaches with abandoned objects.

    Blood that looks slowly through the corner of the eye,                60
made of pressed grass, subterranean nectars.
Blood that rusts the careless trade wind in a trail
and dissolves the butterflies in the panes of the window.

    It is the blood that comes, that will come
over the sheds and rooftops, everywhere,                                      65
to burn the chlorophyll of the blond women,
to groan at the foot of the beds before the insomnia of the
    washbowls
and burst in a low yellow dawn of tobacco.

    One must flee,
flee through the corners and hide on the highest floors,                      70
because the marrow of the forest will penetrate the cracks

to leave in your flesh a light trace of eclipse
and a false sadness of discolored glove and chemical rose.

It is in the wisest silence
when the waiters and the cooks and those who clean with their
        tongues                                                                            75
the wounds of the millionaires
seek their king in the streets and in the corners of the saltpeter.

A wind of wood from the south, oblique in the black mud,
spits upon the broken boats and puts nails in its shoulders;
a south wind that carries                                                          80
fangs, sunflowers, alphabets
and a battery of Volta with smothered wasps.

Oblivion was expressed by three drops of ink upon the
        monocle,
love by a single face invisible on the flower of the stone.
Marrow and corollas composed above the clouds                     85
a desert of sticks without a single rose.

To the left, to the right, in the South and in the North,
an impassive wall is rising
for the mole, the needle of the water.
Do not seek, blacks, its crevice                                               90
to find the infinite mask.
Seek the great sun of the center
having become a humming pineapple.
The sun that slips through the forests
certain of not finding a nymph,                                                  95
the sun that destroys numbers and has never crossed a dream,
the tatooed sun that goes down the river
and bellows, followed by alligators.

Blacks, Blacks, Blacks, Blacks.

Never serpent, or zebra, or mule                                               100
paled upon dying.
The woodcutter does not know when
the clamorous trees he cuts expire.
Wait in the vegetal shade of your king
until hemlock, thistle and nettle disturb your hindermost roofs.   105

Then, blacks, then, then,
you will be able to kiss with frenzy the wheels of the bicycles,

put pairs of microscopes in the caves of the squirrels
and dance, finally, without doubt, while the bristling flowers
assassinate our Moses almost in the bullrushes of heaven.          110

    Oh, Harlem in disguise!
Oh, Harlem, threatened by a crowd of suits without heads!
I hear your murmur,
I hear your murmur going through tree trunks and elevators,
through gray tears,          115
where float their automobiles covered with teeth,
through the dead horses and the small crimes,
through your great desperate king,
whose beard reaches down to the sea.

Supplanting the gypsy as a symbol of natural vitality, the Harlem
Negro becomes for Lorca a tragic expression of the imprisonment of
the blood force of life by the mechanical, depersonalized civilization
which is New York City.[6] "Blood has no doors in your night facing
upwards"; the blood has no outlet, no channels through which to flow
to join man with the natural world. So the volcano will explode, and
the long pent-up energy of the blood—sexuality and natural violence—
will burn the poisonous chlorophyll of the blonds and send fleeing the
white civilization that did not recognize its power. The blood is for
Lorca a spiritual power, the power of the primitive's bond with nature,
the power of the bonds of the unconscious between people who are not
rootless, and the power that flows between the earth and the sky in
men who hold on to both. This is the power that the "friends of the
apple and the sand" have lost.

    Archetypical of the animal world of the tragic vision, as Frye points
out, are "beasts and birds of prey, wolves, vultures, serpents, dragons
and the like."[7] And "Ode to the king of Harlem" opens with a violent
image of crocodiles and monkeys. The crocodile is an ancient, dangerous inhabitant of the swamps and may be associated with a primitive
stage of animal life, as the monkey suggests a primitive stage in the
evolution of human life, a reminder to man of his original animal
nature; both obtain a nightmare aura here in introducing the dark world
of Harlem.

    Line 5 metaphorically forecasts the explosion of the blood force
that is to come, for the flint is like the Harlem Negro in containing a
fire which may be released to bring about a holocaust. It is one of many

images of oppressed or compressed energy that appear throughout the first half of the poem, energy to be released later in the poem: Oppressed eyes (line 32); trembling blood within the dark eclipse (line 33); garnet deaf-mute violence in the shade (line 34); great king prisoner in a janitor's suit (line 35); blood furious beneath the skin (line 54). And this compressed energy will explode, as a volcano explodes, to flood with hot blood the world that has ignored or repressed it.[8] Parallel to this image of contained force is the image of stagnant water (also appearing in the poems "Dawn," p. 497, and "Little girl drowned in the well," p. 504), which suggests that life in New York City no longer seeks the release of its energy.

"Es preciso matar"—"It is necessary to kill." And here (in stanzas 5, 6, and 7) the tone and direction of the poem change. The first four stanzas represent the poet's vision of the world that he passively beholds, a world of violence and agony and stench his conscious mind receives. But then he reacts: he cries out in rage against the white world that has held the black world in chains, and he calls on the blacks to rise up in anger and fight. Accordingly, his language changes from illogical surrealistic images juxtaposed spatially against each other to a more discursive speech that is logically intelligible and is a mandate to action. "It is necessary to kill" all the people of white America who, alienated from each other, live by their overdeveloped cerebral powers, their ego-consciousness, and who prefer the sand (consciousness) to the sea (world of the unconscious and of uninhibited sexual forces). It is necessary to kill them all so that the king of Harlem may sing with his people. For to sing or to chant, the Spanish verb being "cantar," is to try to imitate the rhythms of the universe: chanting effects a lowered level of awareness of the self in isolation and thereby brings about a kind of union on a less-than-conscious level. The Negro community can sing together—the disintegrated white civilization cannot—for the blacks still know the taste of the earth.

After the climax of stanza 7 there is a change of tone, a relief from the high-pitched rhythmical cry of "Oh Harlem! Oh Harlem! Oh Harlem!" The poet's emotion momentarily subsides, so that now he may begin again to describe the moonless night: "The night had a crack. . . ." The image of the whites drinking whiskey, recalling the mandate of line 22, that the blacks must kill the blond seller of whiskey, next to volcanoes, in line 40, forecasts the lava flow of blood that is about to come upon the unaware whites.[9] In fact, the image of the volcano is central to Lorca's vision of the black civilization of Harlem, which is boiling inside with the hot blood of outrage and sexual passion ready to erupt. In the tenth stanza, with the repetition of the opening lines of the poem, the poet once more begins the rhythmical buildup to another climax, another explosion.

"Blacks, Blacks, Blacks, Blacks." The poet repeats the word as a drum would set in motion an orgiastic ritual. Now comes the blood, racing furiously beneath the black skin, ready to explode in a yellow dawn of tobacco smoke. The intensity of the colors black and red increases in the course of the poem as the intensity of passion increases against the colorless civilization that for so long has imprisoned the black. The repetition of the word "Negros" ("Blacks") works to this effect, as does repetition of the word "sangre" ("blood"), until by the end of the poem there seems to be no escape from the blackness of the violent night and the coming flood of red blood. The blood born in the darkness of the earth is the "marrow of the forest," the force of unconscious vitality. This marrow will penetrate the cracks in the white world, in a rape of white flesh, to leave within it "a light trace of eclipse and a false sadness of discolored glove and chemical rose."

After this explosion of energy a calm returns in the third section of the poem, which serves as an ominous prelude to the final stanzas expressing the triumph of the Negroes' rebellion. In silence the black waiters and cooks and those who lick with their tongues the wounds of the millionaires search for their king. A wind from the hot lands of the south blows obliquely in the black mud (suggestive of the primordial state of the earth), as a warning of something to come. This is a desert without a single rose where the memory of life has been lost in the black ink—the written word—on the monocle.[10]

Again (between lines 86 and 87) there is a break, an emptiness waiting to be filled. Now the poet commands the blacks: "Seek the great sun of the center [you] having become a humming pineapple."[11] The image of the "caliente piña" ("hot pineapple") has appeared earlier in the poem (line 21) in connection with the "perfume of the lung" of the "black flush"; so there is already established a relationship between the blacks and the pineapple. (Perhaps the association of the pineapple with the blacks counters the association of the apple with the whites.)[12] The blacks must go towards the hot sun that destroys the lifeless numbers of a mechanical world and goes down the river followed by alligators.

Once more one hears the threatening drumbeat of "Blacks, Blacks, Blacks, Blacks"; and the tension increases. Animals do not pale when they die, says the poet; so the blacks must muster up their courage and await their chance. For finally they shall dance, while the stiffened flowers assassinate "our" Moses almost in the bullrushes of heaven. The allusion is ironic, for Moses led his people out of slavery, but now his people survive by enslaving others—the blacks.

"Oh Harlem, threatened by a crowd of headless suits of clothing!" The poet hears the cry of the oppressed blacks, the rumbling from inside the volcano, across the dead horses (the dead instincts), from their great and desperate king whose beard, a symbol of male potency, reaches down to the sea, the source of life. This final image of the black king's beard contrasts sharply with the numerous images of the rootless, "headless," white civilization floating aimlessly between earth and sky in the "hueco" of the world from which God has fled.[13]

The threat of the "marrow of the forest" reappears in the poem "Danza de la muerte" ("Dance of death," p. 484) in the form of the "mascarón" ("big mask") that comes from Africa to New York and dances.

*The big mask. Look at the big mask!*
*How it comes from Africa to New York!*

The pepper trees went away,
the small buttons of phosphorus.
The camels of torn flesh went away                                             5
and the valleys of light that the swan raised with its beak.

It was the moment of the dry things,
of the wheat in the eye and the laminated cat,
of the iron rust of the big bridges
and the definitive silence of the cork.                                          10

It was the great reunion of the dead animals,
crossed by blades of light;
the eternal happiness of the hippopotamus with hooves of
     ash
and of the gazelle with the immortelle in its throat.

In the withered solitude without end                                    15
the bruised mask was dancing.
Half of the world was of sand,
mercury and sleeping sun the other half.

*The big mask. Look at the big mask!*
*Sand, alligator and fear upon New York!*                               20

Narrow passages of lime imprisoned an empty sky
where the voices of those who die beneath the guano were
     sounding.
A sky cleansed and pure, identical to itself,
with the down and water lily of the invisible mountains,

finished with the lightest sprouts of song                              25
and went away to the packed deluge of sap,
through the repose of the last parades,
lifting with its tail pieces of mirror.

When the chinaman was crying on the roof
without finding the nakedness of his wife                                30
and the director of the bank observing the pressure gauge
that measures the cruel silence of the coin,
the mask was arriving at Wall Street.

It is not strange for the dance
that this columbarium turns its eyes yellow.                             35
From the sphinx to the treasure vault there is a tight thread
that goes through the hearts of the poor children.
The primitive impulse dances with the mechanical impulse,
ignorant in their frenzy of the original light.
Because if the wheel forgets its formula,                                40
it can sing naked with the herds of horses:
and if a flame burns the frozen projects,
the sky will have to flee before the tumult of the windows.

This place is not strange for the dance, I say.
The mask will dance between columns of blood and numbers,                45
between hurricanes of gold and groans of unemployed workers
who will howl, dark night, for your time without lights,
oh savage North America! Oh shame! Oh savage,
stretched out on the frontier of the snow!

*The big mask. Look at the big mask!*                                    50
*What a wave of mud and glow-worm upon New York!*

I was on the terrace fighting with the moon.
Crowds of windows were piercing a thigh of the night.
In my eyes were drinking the sweet cows of the skies.
And the breezes of great wings                                   55
were beating the ash-colored panes of Broadway.

The drop of blood was seeking the light of the bud of the star
to feign a dead apple seed.
The wind of the plain, pushed by the shepherds,
was trembling with the fear of a mollusk without a shell.        60

But it is not the dead men who dance,
I am sure.
The dead men are saturated, devouring their own hands.
It is the others who dance with the mask and his guitar;
it is the others, the drunks of silver, the cold men,            65
those who grow in the crotch of the thighs and hard flames,
those who seek the earthworm in the landscape of the stairs,
those who drink in the bank the tears of the dead little girl
or those who eat on the corners small pyramids of dawn.

Let not the Pope dance!                                          70
No, let not the Pope dance!
Nor the King,
nor the millionaire of blue teeth,
nor the dry dancers of the cathedrals,
nor builders, nor emeralds, nor madmen, nor sodomites.           75
Only this mask,
this mask of old red wool cloth,
only this mask!

For now the cobras will whistle through the highest floors,
for now the nettle will shake patios and terraces,              80
for now the Stock Market will be a pyramid of moss,
for now vines will come after the rifles
and very soon, very soon, very soon.
Oh, Wall Street!

*The big mask. Look at the big mask!*                            85
*How it spits the venom of the jungle*
*on the imperfect anguish of New York!*

The first four quatrains of "Dance of death" present (surrealisti-
cally) the New York world—emptied of pepper trees, dry, and silent—

where in the endless "withered solitude" the black African wearing a mask continues his dance; he brings "sand, alligator and fear upon New York" (line 20). As in the earlier "Ode to the king of Harlem," the reality of the Negro is associated with primitive energy, mysterious darkness, the violence of untamed instincts; and the dangerous forces of this unknown realm are represented by alligators. Herein lies the threat to the sterile world of numbers and machines that is Wall Street.

The quatrains end when the "mascarón" arrives at Wall Street (lines 29-33); and the tenth stanza (lines 34-43) is the longest, being perhaps an expression of the chaos that results from the invasion by the primitive force from the jungle. The "mascarón" gets to Wall Street when the Chinaman is crying because he cannot find his wife's nudity (an image echoing that of the "dressed creatures without nakedness" of the poem "1910") and when the bank director is observing the pressure gauge that "measures the cruel silence of the coin."

> From the sphinx to the treasure vault there is a tight thread
> that goes through the hearts of the poor children.

It is the thread that has joined Africa to New York, and it is this thread upon which the "mascarón" dances.

> The primitive impulse dances with the mechanical impulse,
> ignorant in their frenzy of the original light.

Here is the climax of the poem and of the meeting of Africa and New York: the dance. But somehow this dance is not an imitation of cosmic rhythms. It is not a ritual in which man's unconscious merges ecstatically with the spirit and rhythms of the universe, but rather a frenzy born of the anarchy of a civilization loosed from the earth. "If a flame should burn the frozen projects" of the businessman of Wall Street, "the sky will have to flee before the tumult of the windows" (probably a reference to the suicides that followed the stock market crash of 1929). For the "frozen projects" have replaced the life force in these New York executives; and if these are destroyed, so will be their will to live.

The "mascarón" dances between columns of blood and columns of numbers (line 45) on that taut line between Africa and New York; he dances between groans of unemployed workmen who howl for a night without lights and hurricanes of gold. Here is the meeting place of the jungle and the city, the primitive and the decadent, the blood and the word, the unconscious and the consciousness, the instincts and the projects of New York, the poor who still belong to the earth and the rich who have turned into gold coins. The "mascarón" brings a "wave of mud" to this cold world stretched out on the frontiers of snow.

The poem changes key in line 52 when the poet enters for the first time, and the poem becomes explicitly his vision. The night has an atmosphere of quivering expectancy, as a mollusk without a shell. The dance begins. The "mascarón" has released in the "drunks of silver, the cold men," a latent violence, a primitive fury that now seizes them and holds them helpless in the frenzy. "But let not the Pope dance."

For now comes the apocalypse (in the final climax): "For now the cobras will whistle through the top floors . . . very soon, very soon, very soon." The jungle will take over New York; the snake will wrap itself around the columns of numbers in the offices of the city. Nettle and moss will overcome the patios and terraces and cover the stock market, for vines will take over the earth that was once governed by the rifle.[14] The "mascarón" spits the poison of the jungle upon the imperfect anguish of New York to bring that civilization to its death. As in "Ode to the king of Harlem," "Scream towards Rome," and "Sleepless city," the cataclysmic destruction of the cancer of systematic dehumanization is necessary—and inevitable—before there can be any recovered harmony with the universe.

The climactic rhythm of anguish and outrage, vision and action, in "Ode to the king of Harlem" reappears in "Paisaje de la multitud que vomita" ("Landscape of the vomiting multitude," p. 487), where Lorca expresses the spiritually empty, materially glutted white civilization of New York by the image of the "mujer gorda" ("fat woman") who walks along the city streets "pulling up the roots." Again, the poet first presents his vision, and then establishes his attitude toward this world: "vomit"—a command. The emotion reaches two climaxes, in lines 19 and 29, after which the outrage dies down into resignation as the fat woman continues her walk unperturbed. However, the last line brings a change of tone to the resignation, perhaps even a note of hope, for the entire city is now crowding toward the railings of the pier. Are they there to vomit?

The fat woman was coming forward
pulling up the roots and wetting the parchment of the drums;
the fat woman
who turns inside out the agonizing octopuses.
The fat woman, enemy of the moon,                                          5
was running through the deserted streets and apartments
and was leaving in the corners small pigeon skulls
and was rousing the furies of the banquets of the last centuries
and was calling the demon of bread on the corners of the swept
      sky
and was filtering an ardent desire of light into the subterranean
      traffic.                                                                     10
It is the cemeteries, I know, it is the cemeteries
and the pain of the kitchens buried beneath the sand,
it is the dead, the pheasants and the apples of another hour
that push up into our throats.

The sounds of the jungle of vomit were arriving                            15
with the empty women, with children of hot wax,
with fermented trees and untiring waiters
who serve plates of salt beneath the harps of the saliva.
There is nothing else to do, my son, vomit! There is nothing
      else to do.
It is not the vomit of the highway robbers over the breasts of
      the prostitute,                                                            20
nor is it the vomit of the cat that swallowed a frog accidentally.
It is the dead who scratch with their hands of earth
the doors of flint where clouds and desserts are rotting.

The fat woman was coming forward
with the people from the boats, from the taverns and from the
      gardens.                                                                    25
The vomit stirred delicately their drums
among some little girls of blood
who were asking the moon for protection.
Oh! Oh! Oh!
This gaze of mine was mine, but now it is not mine,                        30
this gaze that trembles naked from the alcohol
and says goodby to incredible boats
on the anemones of the piers.
I defend myself with this gaze
that comes from the waves where the dawn dares not venture,               35

I, poet, without arms, lost
midst the multitude that is vomiting,
without an effusive horse that might cut
the thick mosses from my temples.

But the fat woman was continuing forward                    40
and the people were seeking the pharmacies
where the tropical bitters are fixed.
Only when they raised the flag and the first dogs arrived
the entire city crowded at the railings of the pier.

With a yank the "fat woman" uproots plants, so that they may no
longer participate in the productive cycle of nature.[15] The image of the
rootless plant is the converse of the tree stump: as the plant is no longer
joined to the earth, the tree stump is no longer joined to the heavens.
The uprooted plant thus becomes a symbol of this modern dissociated
society in which man has lost connection with the nutritive forces of
the earth and of the unconscious of his race. The fat woman wets the
parchments of the drums; now they cannot sound or make the music
that would unite the community in a subconscious communication
beyond words, before words. Rupert Allen, in a discussion of another
poem, has pointed out that the tambourine is an incantatory instru-
ment which reduces consciousness (self-consciousness) in a community
of human beings to bring the group or tribe to a subconscious, non-
verbal communion of ritual, dancing.[16] Here there is no escape from
consciousness, from isolating subjectivity. An apocalypse, however, is a
means of reducing consciousness, of bringing civilization face to face
with the overwhelmingly destructive unleashed forces of nature.

The fat woman is an enemy of the moon, which is normally
associated not only with woman but also with death as part of nature's
cycle. And perhaps the disharmony between the fat woman and the
moon is another allusion to sleeplessness, excessive consciousness. This
fat woman, repulsive, overfed, dehumanized, is not in harmony with
the forces and rhythms of the universe, but rather is an unnatural force
of devitalized materialism which robs the society of its ties with the
earth and the heavens. She leaves the skulls of "palomas" ("doves" or
"pigeons") in the corners of old deserted apartments, as she leaves the
skeleton of Christianity—the spirit having gone—in the vacant buildings
that she visits.

Something is making "our" civilization nauseated (lines 11-14); it is the accumulation of the centuries, the dead, the "apples of another hour"—the accumulated knowledge, consciousness—that is now too much. It is the accumulation of the material without a unifying spiritual tradition to make the whole meaningful. The woman has overeaten. Vomit! The apple of knowledge is killing the forces of life, and we must vomit to get the poison out of our system. That is the only way out.

Now (in line 30) the poet enters his poem, which narrows suddenly to become his personal anguished cry. He continues to cry out, although his cry issues from within dark waves, his arms have been amputated by a world that threatens his spirit, and he is lost in the vomiting multitude, in the sea without a horse (the vital force, the libido, with which the sea might have saved him). This drowning image, one of many, represents the impotent poet who no longer feels that he is a creative force speaking the feelings of all mankind. His hands, his means of expression and his possibility for embracing the world and the rest of mankind, have been severed by a hostile society.

The fat woman continues her walk, wandering alone through the empty streets, a symbol of modern civilization for which the taking of food is no longer a ritual.[17] As man is alienated from food production, from the wheat growing in the fields, so is he alienated from communal food consumption, the ritual by which men's lives were once joined to each other and to the processes of nature by which men participated in the "periodical renewal of the World" and the periodical renewal of their spirit.[18] Thus the fat woman goes alone through the city, empty of spirit, empty of meaning, unrelated to the rhythms and cycles of nature.

And yet "when they raised the banner and the first dogs arrived the entire city crowded at the railings of the pier." Why? Is it to leave, or is it to vomit, as the poet has said they must to purge themselves of all they have taken in and to prepare themselves for something new? Perhaps there is hope. "Landscape of the vomiting multitude," like "Ode to the king of Harlem," follows the rhythm of tragedy in that the universe, by a cosmic upheaval, must expel the evil within that is its cancer. This is the rhythm of the cyclic renewal of the world by which death precedes rebirth, winter precedes spring; and it is the rhythm of the Christian cycle. The poet recognizes such symbolic death—the flood of blood, the act of vomiting, revolution—as necessary before any spiritual rebirth may take place. Lorca sees the loss of ritual and myth as central to the disintegration of the community, which is slowly dying, unaware of its cancer. The whole power of his poetry goes toward "forcing the moment to its crisis" (in Eliot's words) out of its inertia, so that there may be a cataclysmic convulsion, a violent purgation leading to renewal: death and resurrection. The passive-active rhythm of many of his poems is an expression of the cosmic rhythm of periodical renewal and therefore ultimately an expression of the poet's alignment with nature.

A prophetic vision of destructive chaos from which issues a new harmony occurs in "Ciudad sin sueño" ("Sleepless city," p. 492), which also falls into the fundamental climactic arrangement that Susanne Langer calls the tragic rhythm of self-consummation.[19] The poem follows the order of (1) description of the horror (lines 1-21); (2) prophecy of destruction (lines 22-25); (3) vision of a new life of wholeness and harmony (lines 26-29); (4) mandate to destroy the horror (lines 30-37); and (5) return to the mood of the poem's opening lines. The cycle is that of the myth of descent into darkness and chaos and then ascent into light and harmony. The final stanza, after the climax of the passionate outburst of the fourth and fifth stanzas, returns to the passivity of the poet's response at the beginning.

Nobody sleeps in the sky. Nobody, nobody.
Nobody sleeps.
The creatures of the moon sniff and circle the cabins.
The live iguanas will come to bite the men who do not dream
and he who flees with his heart broken will encounter on the
    corners                                 5
the incredible crocodile quiet beneath the tender protest of the
    stars.

Nobody sleeps in the world. Nobody, nobody.
Nobody sleeps.
There is a dead man in the most distant cemetery
who complains for three years                            10
because he has a dry landscape on his knee;
and the child they buried this morning was crying so much
that it was necessary to call the dogs so that he would be still.

Life is not a dream. Beware! Beware! Beware!
We fall down the stairs to eat the humid earth                                    15
or we climb to the edge of the snow with the chorus of dead
        dahlias.
But there is no forgetting, or dreaming:
live flesh. Kisses tie mouths together
in a jungle of recent veins
and he whose pain hurts him will ache without rest                                 20
and he who fears death will carry it upon his shoulders.

    One day
horses will live in the taverns
and furious ants
will attack the yellow skies that take refuge in the eyes of the
        cows.                                                                       25

    Another day
we shall see the resurrection of the dissected butterflies
and even walking through a landscape of gray sponges and mute
        boats
we shall see our ring shining and roses flowing from our tongue.
Beware! Beware! Beware!                                                            30
Those who still keep watch over the tracks of paw and heavy
        shower,
that boy who cries because he does not know the invention of the
        bridge
or that dead man that now has nothing more than his head and
        a shoe—
they must be carried to the wall where iguanas and serpents wait,
where the teeth of the bear wait,                                                  35
where the mummified hand of the child waits
and the skin of the camel bristles with a violent blue shiver.

    Nobody sleeps in the sky. Nobody, nobody.
Nobody sleeps.
But if someone closes his eyes,                                                    40
beat him, my sons, beat him!
There is a panorama of open eyes
and bitter burning wounds.
Nobody sleeps in the world. Nobody, nobody.
Now I have spoken.                                                                 45
Nobody sleeps.

But if someone has in the night an excess of moss on his temples,
open the trap doors so that he may see beneath the moon
the false goblets, the venom and the skull of the theaters.

Sleeplessness serves as a metaphor for agonizing, inescapable consciousness in "Sleepless city." To sleep would be to lose consciousness,
to fall into temporal harmony with the universe; and it would mean to
be in touch with the spiritually regenerative forces of the unconscious,
individual and collective. But to be sleepless is to be locked into the
eye-open consciousness of the isolated subjectivity.[20] Vision implies
separation: the eye that sees is separated from what it sees, as the seeing
self is conscious of the world outside it. When the self has become so
conscious that it withdraws from the world by making the world (God)
an object of its perception, then it no longer can find rest in the earth.

Before the self was fragmented, the ego lived in harmony with the
unconscious; now, when man has suppressed or ignored the instincts of
the blood, the unconscious will rebel.

The live iguanas will come to bite the men who do not dream
and the one who flees with his heart broken will meet on the corners
the incredible crocodile quiet beneath the tender protest of the stars.

Those who do not sleep, who do not dream, will suffer the revolt of the
primitive forces of the unconscious. These demonic animals from the
world of the nightmare foretell anarchy and destruction for the world
which has ignored the realm that gave it birth.

In the unnatural civilization of New York City even the dead cannot
lose consciousness: the dead man in the cemetery complains for three
years because he has a landscape on his knee (lines 9-11); and the child
they buried this morning would not stop crying until they called the
dogs (lines 12-13). Life is not a dream: there is no escape from reality,
no relief from its pain. The fear of death leads to a death-in-life, a
"waste land." In line 22 the description of this reality suddenly becomes a prophecy of apocalypse: one day the "waste land" of this
mechanized, fragmented society will be torn apart by the "horses" and
"furious ants," the subhuman destructive forces of the unconscious
which will take revenge.

The prophetic vision of lines 22 through 25 recalls the Apocalypse
of the Book of Revelation, where "those men which have not the seal

of God in their foreheads" suffer "hail and fire mingled with blood" and a plague of locusts; "and the shapes of the locusts were like unto horses prepared unto battle."[21]

5   And to them it was given that they should not kill them, but that they should be tormented five months: and their torment was as the torment of a scorpion, when he striketh a man.
6   And in those days shall men seek death, and shall not find it; and shall desire to die, and death shall flee from them.[22]

This is the curse of consciousness. When the apocalypse comes, there is no escape, not even in death. Yet after the scourge,

we shall see the resurrection of the dissected butterflies
and even walking through a landscape of gray sponges and mute boats
we shall see our ring shining and roses flowing from our tongue.

After death there is resurrection: after the violent destruction there is a new life, a new wholeness. The butterfly (which once symbolized the poet's heart and spirit, p. 190), which was drowned in the inkwell in the first poem of *Poet in New York* and dissected by the dehumanized intellect of modern civilization, is now resurrected. The perfect wholeness and love suggested by the shining ring and the "roses flowing from our tongue" form a beatific state reminiscent of Dante's paradise. And so Lorca's lines 27 through 29 echo the spirit of Revelation, after the Apocalypse: "And I saw a new heaven and a new earth: for the first heaven and the first earth were passed away; and there was no more sea."[23]

After the vision of perfect unity and harmony the poem returns to the present reality of unrelieved consciousness in which "nobody sleeps"; but now the poet will not let us close our eyes, for we must take it all in. For only by going all the way into the fullest consciousness can this civilization purge itself of the evil forces within and emerge to a new life; only by leaving the twilight world of incomplete anguish and passing through the "dark night," confronting the hostile iguanas and serpents of the unconscious, can we hope to be redeemed. Here can be seen the tragic rhythm of the individual life that sees its destiny and fulfills it. The universe likewise fulfills its destiny by undergoing an apocalyptic convulsion in order to destroy and expel the cancer within, so that it may continue its existence.

Sleeplessness, the curse of consciousness, reappears in "La aurora" ("Dawn," p. 497), which presents another vision of the modern world wherein the light has been buried—"La luz es sepultada."

The dawn of New York has
four columns of mud
and a hurricane of black doves
that dabble in the rotten waters.

The dawn of New York groans                                          5
along the immense stairs
seeking between the ledges
nards of anguish sketched.

The dawn arrives and nobody receives it in his mouth
because there there is no morning or hope possible.              10
At times the coins in furious crowds
penetrate and devour abandoned children.

The first ones who come out understand with their bones
that there will not be any paradise or leafless loves;
they know that they go to the bog of numbers and laws,          15
to the games without art, to the sweat without fruit.

The light is buried by chains and noises
in the impudent threat of knowledge without roots.
In the neighborhoods there are people who stagger sleepless
as if recently emerged from a disaster of blood.                20

Dawn is blocked not only by "four columns of mud," the sky-scrapers of New York, but also by "a hurricane of black doves" which drink the "rotten waters" of the city. The white dove traditionally represents the Holy Ghost, but it has vanished from the skies over New York; in its stead is the black dove soiled by civilization. The rotten waters refer superficially to New York's polluted waters, while representing metaphorically the stain and corruption of man's unconscious. The water that has been the source of all life has become polluted. And when the waters are "rotten," they are no longer "fruitful for the regeneration of men"; they may no longer be the "immaculate womb" which gave birth to Christ and thereby made possible man's own spiritual rebirth through baptism.[24] Instead of the Holy Ghost moving on the face of the waters, sanctifying them, the black doves dabble in the stinking ponds. Dawn should mean a renewal of the spirit, but here nobody receives it "in his mouth." Lorca's phrase "recibe en la boca" is probably an ironic allusion to Holy Communion, which is not a part of this secular world that has no sacred time and space. The sun (which often symbolizes a god) cannot penetrate the smog and therefore cannot bring hope: there is no morning or hope possible.

Money becomes the active force in this world, where "the coins in furious crowds penetrate and devour abandoned children." The bog of numbers and laws has replaced paradise. The mud that blocked the dawn and polluted the air (in line 2) and waters, making impossible spiritual rebirth, is the hell of the civilization separated from its gods, from nature. There is no art, for art must contain the seed of a spiritual vision; and light is buried in chains and noises. Man's original harmony with the world has been replaced by a "knowledge without roots," a consciousness no longer held fast to the earth. Nobody can sleep in this world of extreme consciousness: there is no relief from vision.

In "New York: Oficina y denuncia" ("New York: Office and denunciation," p. 515), the poet offers himself as the sacrificial lamb desperately needed by the civilization of rootless knowledge represented by New York.

> Beneath the multiplications
> there is a drop of duck's blood;
> beneath the divisions
> there is a drop of sailor's blood;
> beneath the sums, a river of young blood; 5
> A river that comes singing
> through the bedrooms of the suburbs,
> and it is silver, cement, or breeze
> in the false dawn of New York.
> Mountains exist. I know. 10
> And glasses for higher learning.
> I know. But I have not come to see the sky.
> I have come to see the turbid blood.
> The blood that carries the machines to the waterfalls
> and the spirit to the snake's tongue. 15
> Everyday there are killed in New York
> four million ducks,
> five million pigs,

two thousand pigeons for the pleasure of the dying,
one million cows,                                                    20
one million lambs
and two million roosters,
that leave the sky in smithereens.
It is better to sob sharpening the knife
or murder the dogs                                                   25
in the fascinating hunts,
than to endure in the early morning
the interminable milk trains,
the interminable trains of blood
and the trains of handcuffed roses                                   30
for the merchants of perfume.
The ducks and the pigeons,
and the pigs and the lambs
leave their drops of blood
beneath the multiplications,                                         35
and the terrible bawling of the jammed-together cows
fills the valley with pain
where the Hudson gets drunk on oil.
I denounce all the people
who are ignorant of the other half,                                  40
I denounce the irredeemable half
that raises its mountains of cement
where beat the hearts
of animals now forgotten
and where we all shall fall                                          45
in the last feast of the blasting drills,
I spit in your face.
The other half listens to me
devouring, urinating, flying in their purity,
like the children of the doorways                                    50
who carry old sticks
to the holes where are rusting
the antennae of insects.
It is not hell, it is the street.
It is not death, it is the fruit store.                              55
There is a world of broken rivers
and unreachable distances
in the paw of that cat
broken by the automobile,
and I hear the song of the earthworm                                 60

in the hearts of many little girls.
Rust, rot, shuddering earth.
Earth, yourself, who swim
through the numbers of the office.
What shall I do? Set the landscape in order?                    65
Set in order the loves that will later be photographs,
that will later be pieces of wood
and mouthfuls of blood?
St. Ignatius of Loyola
murdered a small rabbit                                        70
and still his lips grieve
in the towers of the churches.
No, no, no, no; I denounce.
I denounce the conspiracy
of these deserted offices                                      75
that do not radiate agony,
that erase the programs of the jungle,
and I offer up myself to be eaten
by the jammed-together cows
when their bawling fills the valley                            80
where the Hudson gets drunk on oil.

A line-by-line analysis of the poem would not be particularly useful, as the many images of the city need not be explained for their symbolic implications to be understood. However, the form of the poem as a whole significantly reflects the conflict between "multiplicity" and "unity" which constitutes one of its themes. A Whitmanian enumeration of animals killed every day in New York stylistically supports the image of vast numbers which Lorca uses to describe the city. The "multiplications" (line 1) and "divisions" (line 3) express a disintegrating world no longer unified by a central myth in which all might believe: this is the world of relativity, where the heavens have been left in pieces (line 23).[25]

In this poem Lorca identifies himself with the "one drop of duck's blood" that lies "beneath the multiplications"; with the "drop of sailor's blood" that lies "beneath the divisions"; with the "river of young blood" that lies "beneath the sums." So the poet continually counters abstract multiplicity with the oneness of blood (symbolic of life, sexual energy, and violent death); and he says, "I have come to see the turbid blood" (line 13). It is blood that all men (animals) have in common and that ultimately will flood the dehumanized world of machines in a violent purging torrent.

The poet lists the animals that are slaughtered daily by the inhabitants of New York in ironic sacrifice to this mechanical civilization: two thousand pigeons, the dove representing the Holy Ghost; one million cows, the cow suggesting fertility, the moon, and nature; one million lambs, the lamb symbolizing Christ as a sacrifice; two million roosters, the rooster also recalling the death of Christ. These animals "put their drops of blood beneath the multiplications" as a sacrifice to the fragmented heavens.

And "the Hudson gets drunk on oil" (line 38); the Hudson River is polluted.[26] The waters which once brought life now being death; the water which once served to baptize man to renewed spiritual life can now only reflect his spiritual death. And the oil which was a symbol of healing and mercy in the Bible has become the oil of automobiles and machines, carrying man away from God.

Lorca denounces this civilization of New York City and identifies himself with "the other half," the more primitive world of Spain, its streets and fruitstands. Beneath all the multiplications he can hear the song of the earthworm in the hearts of the children. In this poem, one of the last poems in the volume, Lorca knows who he is and where he belongs. He belongs to the blood and to the world of the downtrodden being murdered by the dehumanized civilization of the city.

"What shall I do? Set the landscape in order? . . . No, no, no, no; I denounce."[27] And identifying with the sacrificed animals and the drop of sailor's blood, Lorca offers himself as a sacrifice in order that his blood may merge with the "river of young blood" in a passionate protest against the "conspiracy of these deserted offices that do not radiate agony." This wish for death and for vital participation in nature is a symbolic self-sacrifice, that another kind of world may be born of the blood shed in this one. Again, as in "Ode to the king of Harlem" and "Scream towards Rome," the poet sees the absence of ritual, a consequence of which is the absence of passion, as instrumental in the fragmentation of life in New York City; without ritual there is nothing to hold the society together. The meaningless world grows abstract: "multiplications," "divisions," "sums. . . ." The world needs an apocalypse. In the dramatic confrontation between images of "multiplicity" and images of "unity" (that is, the image of the blood), the poet embraces "unity." For the poet who seemed to have lost his identity in "Return from a walk" has recovered it. No longer a victim, he offers himself, by his own choice, as the sacrificial lamb so desperately needed for mankind's salvation.

In 1918, in *Libro de poemas*, Lorca wrote,

> And the song of the water
> is something eternal.
>
> . . . . . . . . . . . . . . . . . .
> It is the blood of poets
> who let their souls
> lose themselves on the paths
> of nature.
>
> (p. 192)

In 1930 Lorca writes in "Oda a Walt Whitman" ("Ode to Walt Whitman," p. 522), "you dreamed of being a river and sleeping as a river." And it is for this quality, the merging with the rhythms of nature, time, and blood, becoming at once individual man and all mankind, that Lorca praises Walt Whitman. The American bard whose poetry flowed from the depths of his own soul and of his whole race, and who said, "I salute all the inhabitants of the earth," is the "virginal Apollo" (line 32) whom Lorca sees as a god among men. "Ode to Walt Whitman," one of the final poems of *Poet in New York*, is a tribute to the greatness of the poet who rises above small men who do not dream of being a river or a cloud (lines 7 and 17).

> Along the East River and the Bronx,
> the young men were singing showing their waists,
> with the wheel, the oil, the leather and the hammer.
> Ninety thousand miners were taking silver out of the rocks
> and the boys were drawing ladders and perspectives.          5
>
> But nobody was sleeping,
> nobody wanted to be the river,
> nobody loved the large leaves,
> nobody loved the blue tongue of the beach.
>
> Along the East River and Queensborough                       10
> the young men were fighting with industry,

and the jews were selling to the faun of the river
the rose of the circumcision
and the sky emptied over the bridges and the roofs
herds of bison pushed by the wind.                                         15

    But nobody was stopping,
nobody wanted to be a cloud,
nobody was seeking the ferns
or the yellow wheel of the drum.

    When the moon comes out                                     20
the pulleys will turn to disturb the sky;
a border of needles will enclose the memory
and the coffins will carry off those who do not work.

    New York of mud,
New York of wire and death.                                                25
What angel do you carry hidden in your cheek?
What perfect voice will speak the truths of the wheat?
Who will speak the terrible dream of the stained anemones?

    Not a single moment, old beautiful Walt Whitman,
have I stopped seeing your beard full of butterflies,                       30
or your shoulders of corduroy wasted by the moon,
or your muscles of a virginal Apollo,
or your voice like a column of ash;
old man beautiful as the cloud
who cried like a bird                                                       35
with his sex pierced by a needle,
enemy of the satyr,
enemy of the vine
and lover of bodies under the heavy cloth.
Not a single moment, virile beauty                                         40
who on mountains of carbon, advertisements and railroads,
dreamed of being a river and sleeping as a river
with that comrade who would put in your breast
a small pain of an unknowing leopard.

    Not a single moment, Adam of blood, male,                   45
lone man in the sea, old beautiful Walt Whitman,
for on the rooftops,
clustered in the bars,
leaving in bunches from the sewers

trembling between the legs of the chauffeurs                                50
or turning around on platforms of wormwood,
the perverts, Walt Whitman, dreamed of you.

Also that! As well! And they fling themselves
upon your luminous and chaste beard,
blonds from the north, blacks from the sand,                                55
crowds of shouts and gestures,
like cats and like serpents,
the perverts, Walt Whitman, the perverts
turbid with tears, flesh for the whiplash,
boot or bite of the animal trainers.                                        60

Also that! As well! Stained fingers
point to the bank of your dream
when the friend eats your apple
with a light taste of gasoline
and the sun sings through the navels                                        65
of the young men who play beneath the bridges.

But you were not seeking scratched eyes,
or the dark bog where they submerge the boys,
or the frozen saliva,
or the curves wounded like a toad's belly                                   70
that the perverts carry in cars and on terraces
while the moon lashes them on the corners of terror.

You were seeking a nude who might be like a river,
bull and dream that might unite the wheel and the seaweed,
father of your agony, camelia of your death,                                75
who would cry in the flames of your hidden equator.

For it is just that man not seek his pleasure
in the jungle of blood of the following morning.
The sky has beaches for the evasion of life
and there are bodies that should not be repeated at dawn.                   80

Agony, agony, dream, ferment and dream.
This is the world, friend, agony, agony.
The dead decompose beneath the clock of the cities,
the war passes crying with a million gray rats,
the rich give to their mistresses                                          85
small lighted dying ones,
and life is not noble, or good, or sacred.

Man can, if he wants, conduct his desire
through the coral vein or celestial nude.
Tomorrow the loves will be rocks and Time                    90
a breeze that comes sleeping through the branches.

Therefore I do not raise my voice, old Walt Whitman,
against the boy who writes
the name of a girl on his pillow,
nor against the youth who dresses as a bride              95
in the darkness of the closet,
nor against the lonely men of the casinos
who drink with nausea the water of prostitution,
nor against the men with the green gaze
who love men and burn their lips in silence.              100
But I do raise my voice against you, perverts of the cities,
of swelling flesh and filthy thought,
mothers of mud, harpies, sleepless enemies
of the Love that distributes wreaths of joy.

Against you always, who give to the young men       105
drops of filthy death with bitter venom.
Against you always,
*Faeries* of North America,
*Pájaros* of Havana,
*Jotos* of Mexico,                                       110
*Sarasas* of Cadiz,
*Apios* of Seville,
*Cancos* of Madrid,
*Floras* of Alicante,
*Adelaidas* of Portugal.                                 115

Perverts everywhere, assassins of doves!
Slaves of the woman, bitches of their boudoirs,
open in the plazas with fan fever
or ambushed in motionless landscapes of hemlock.

May there be no district! Death                          120
flows from your eyes
and groups gray flowers on the bank of the mud.
May there be no district! Watch out!
That the confused, the pure,
the classic, the distinguished, the entreating ones     125
may shut the doors of the bacchanal.

And you, handsome Walt Whitman, sleep on the rivers of
    the Hudson
with your beard towards the pole and your hands open.
Soft clay or snow, your tongue is calling
comrades to watch your disembodied gazelle.             130
Sleep, nothing remains.
A dance of walls shakes the meadows
and America is flooded in machines and sobs.
I want the strong air of the deepest night
to take away flowers and letters from the arch where you
    sleep                            135
and a black child to announce to the whites of the gold
the coming of the reign of the wheat.

Whitman's homosexuality is not that of the "maricas" ("perverts")
of all the cities against whom Lorca raises his voice (line 101), but
rather the purer love of a universal brotherhood. It is Whitman whose
beard is "full of butterflies" (line 30), of poetry, who becomes an
"Adam of blood" (line 45) to stand alone in the sea (line 46), a giant
among men. Whitman, who "sleeps on the banks of the Hudson with
his beard towards the pole and his hands open" (lines 127-128), should
continue sleeping, for his America is now drowning in machines and
tears (lines 131-133).

Nevertheless, the poem is also an ode to the agonized souls whose
homosexuality yields them only the pain of frustrated love, and Lorca
does not raise his voice against them (lines 93-100). For they are
alienated human beings for whom there is no place in the world and
who—like the poet of "Nocturne of the void"—know the anguish of
unfulfilled longing.

The style of this ode is itself Whitmanian: the repetitive parallel
construction of the clauses (as in lines 6-9 and 16-19), the lyrical-narra-
tive nature of the long lines, the lists of concrete specifics representing
universals. But beyond this style is the coincidence of the two poets'
attitude toward humanity, their common identification with the downtrodden. Whitman writes in "Salut au Monde,"

> I see all the menials of the earth, laboring,
> I see all the prisoners in the prisons,
> I see the defective human bodies of the earth,

The blind, the deaf and dumb, idiots, hunchbacks, lunatics,

. . . . . . . . . . . . . . . . . . . . . . . . . . . . . . .

And I salute all the inhabitants of the earth.

Like Whitman, Lorca is the voice of the poor. By the end of his stay in New York City, Lorca knows that a revolution must come in which the poor will rise up against the rich and demand their share of the fruits of the earth—as in "the will of the Earth that gives its fruits for all" (p. 522). "Scream towards Rome" and "Ode to Walt Whitman" both conclude with an invocation that "the reign of the wheat" (symbolizing fertility) may come, that the earth will share her bread with all. Lorca's identification with Whitman is an identification with the force of the blood, the natural world.

In the three poems, "New York: Office and denunciation," "Scream towards Rome," and "Ode to Walt Whitman," Lorca's language reflects his renewed harmonious relationship with the rhythms of nature. Gone are the surrealistic images of the earlier poems created when he was alienated from everything outside his subjectivity. His language has become simpler, less "spatial," indeed more rhythmical, for the poet has recovered his lost self. The increasingly harmonious relationship reaches its climax in "Son de negros en Cuba" ("Sound of blacks in Cuba," p. 530), written when the poet visits Havana after leaving New York City.[28] The entire poem has the incantatory rhythm of the beating of drums. Moving away from the medium of painting, which the first poems in the volume approached, this poetry approaches the medium of music, indicating acceptance of the world and time.

. . . This is a new age which seeks to reduce everything to uniformity in the realm of matter while it tends to shatter all universality in the realm of the spirit in deference to an anarchistic individualism.[29]

                                                            Igor Stravinsky

The loss of a unifying myth has led to a world of relative values which simultaneously threatens man's identity and fails to provide a cohesive community through which he might know where he belongs in the universe (or, more simply, that he belongs in the universe). The absence of "all universality in the realm of the spirit" has meant a reduction of human society to purposelessness. The poet envisions an apocalyptic self-destruction as necessary and inevitable before the sick civilization can regain health and harmony with the cosmos; and this "baptism," cataclysmic as it may be, makes hope possible.

Richard Saez compares this volume of Lorca's poetry to Eliot's *The Waste Land* in sharing common allegories of death and rebirth.[30] "The sickness of New York," says Saez, "is that the sacrifice, which the natural cycle of events demands, is not made ritually or ceremonially." With Saez's hypothesis, I am in basic agreement; but with his proof, in which, for example, he views Negroes as suffering creatures who hate conflict rather than as representatives of the blood force who will overcome the sterile "waste land," I am in disagreement. For Saez, Lorca's crisis has been a loss of faith, finally recovered in "New York: Office and denunciation," in which the poet is reconciled with the city and has attained a "maturer belief." The means of this reconciliation is his poetry, "the life-giving waters themselves, which ultimately execute and give meaning to, or mythologize, the ritual sacrifice," thus setting his lands in order.[31] According to this point of view, then, Lorca's *Poet in New York* would be the "fragments [he has] shored against [his] ruin," the order he has made out of the chaos to effect his own salvation.

However, this personal redemption is not the implication of Lorca's line, for after posing the question "What shall I do? Set the landscape in order?" he says, "No, no, no, no; I denounce." Lorca and Eliot see the same "waste land," but their reactions to it differ radically. Eliot sets his lands in order by shaping the fragments into a poem, into art; thus his quest is for a personal salvation which takes place within his own consciousness, independent of the chaos he beholds. Lorca, on the other hand, refuses to accept the disorder passively. If he is indeed alluding to Eliot's response, then he is giving a different solution: revolt. The separation of the poet from the world inherent in Eliot's attitude at the end of *The Waste Land*, a separation reflected in the spatial form of the poem, is not found in Lorca's final "engagement" in the world in which he identifies himself with the force of the blood and rebels against the forces of evil that are destroying the wholeness of the community.

Lorca's journey is from separation to union; that is, from total alienation and loss of self, as revealed in the first poem of the volume, "Return from a walk," to recovery of self and identification with the blood force. Just as many of the individual poems follow the climactic arrangement of vision-action, the work as a whole expresses such a rhythm of separation (implied by vision) and reconciliation, so that by the end of the book the poet has become one with "the will of the Earth that gives its fruits for all." Now the poet is finally at "the centre," moving in time with the drums of the Negroes in Cuba, in temporal harmony with the world, as is revealed in the book's final poem, "Son de negros en Cuba" ("Sound of blacks in Cuba," p. 530).

> When the full moon arrives
> I shall go to Santiago, Cuba.
> I shall go to Santiago
> in a coach of black water.
> I shall go to Santiago.                                     5
> The palm roofs will sing.
> I shall go to Santiago.
> When the palm wants to be stork.
> I shall go to Santiago.
> And when the banana wants to be medusa.                     10
> I shall go to Santiago.
> With the blond head of Fonseca.
> I shall go to Santiago.
> And with the rose of Romeo and Juliet.
> I shall go to Santiago.                                     15
> Paper sea and silver coins.
> I shall go to Santiago.
> Oh Cuba, oh rhythm of dry seeds!
> I shall go to Santiago.
> Oh hot waist and drop of wood!                              20
> I shall go to Santiago
> Harp of live trunks, alligator, tobacco flower!
> I shall go to Santiago.
> I always said I would go to Santiago
> in a coach of black water.                                  25
> I shall go to Santiago.
> Breeze and alcohol in the wheels.
> I shall go to Santiago.
> My coral in the darkness.
> I shall go to Santiago.                                     30
> The sea drowned in the sand.
> I shall go to Santiago.

White heat, dead fruit.
I shall go to Santiago.
Oh bovine fresh air of canefields!                    35
Oh Cuba! Oh curve of breath and clay!
I shall go to Santiago.

# Chapter Five

# Conclusion

Federico García Lorca's *Poet in New York* attracted attention when published in the early 1940s as a strange, impenetrable work, apparently surrealist in origin, which seemed to represent a rejection of the traditional style of his earlier poetry and an embarkation upon a new experiment in poetic creation. The "experiment" was regarded by many as a failure: the poetry somehow did not measure up to the greatness of either *Libro de poemas* or the later *Diván del Tamarit*. Our examination of the imagery of *Poet in New York* has shown that its poetic process is not essentially different from that of *Libro de poemas* and *Canciones*; that the New York poetry is a symbolic expression of the poet's state of mind, as is his earlier work. The striking revolution evident here, therefore, is not a basic change of technique (as it would be if the poet were adopting the surrealist aesthetic), but rather a change of form, revealing the poet's sudden alienation from society and nature. The new "style" records the shock of the poet's confrontation with a hostile world and the depression he suffers from his isolation within it.

*Poet in New York* is an account of a journey from alienation and disorientation toward regained identification with the force of the blood and a harmonious relationship with the universe. The journey is expressed in the poetic form, which develops from "spatial" to "temporal," as the poet moves from a passivity in which he can only name the violent forces battering his subjectivity toward a participation in nature in which he can now act.

The metaphor inherent in the poet's alienation is the Fall. Having once known harmony, man is condemned by his consciousness to seek it forever, for his consciousness brings into being the knowledge of absence, the "hueco." In *Poet in New York* the "hueco" expands to include far more than the poet's personal feelings of separation and emptiness; it becomes the very condition of modern man wrenched free from nature by his destructive intellect. New York City is, for Lorca, a concrete symbol of this state of "consciousness" and of the disintegration of the community resulting from man's estrangement from nature.

Primitive man reaffirmed his original relationship with nature periodically by such communal ceremonies as the ritual sacrifice which made regeneration possible; modern man, no longer belonging to a spiritually united community, but rather living in a world of relative values, does not participate in such rites. Instead, modern man, as Lorca sees him, exists in a world of "imperfect anguish," out of touch with either the earth or the heavens, unacquainted with death, unaware of his own spiritual decay. Again and again in these poems this anguish of incompleteness reaches a climax in some kind of apocalypse. It is either a symbolic societal sacrifice, as in the flood of blood the poet calls for, or a symbolic personal self-sacrifice to bridge the abyss between the self and God, between the self and nature. This sacrifice is the means whereby the poet is finally reintegrated into nature to move in time with the rhythms of the cosmos, as he does in the concluding poems "Waltz in the branches" and "Sound of blacks in Cuba." Thus *Poet in New York* may be viewed as a soul's symbolic journey from Adam to Christ, with Adam becoming Christ through the sacrifice.

The poet as Adam—expelled from the Garden, condemned to self-consciousness and endless longing for a beyond—is implicit in the imagery, theme, and style of most of *Poet in New York*. Such is the meaning of the "tree trunk that does not sing," the "poet without arms," the "knowledge without roots," the "hollows," the sleeplessness. Such is the meaning of the poem "Muerte" ("Death," p. 506), which expresses a desire for stasis, freedom from the agonizing cycle of continual change born of the sense of incompleteness which is "desire." The Fall is the metaphor at the root of the spatial form of the surrealistic language, which presents a chaotic, unintelligible world of things bombarding the alienated poet. The fragmentation of the world apparent in the poem "Return from a walk" is a reflection of the poet's loss of identity, since in his extreme isolation the poet cannot perceive any wholeness to a world existing outside his subjectivity.

The tension created by this state of consciousness, manifest throughout *Poet in New York* in its images, themes, and form, is, in fact, the tension born of incompleteness; it therefore generates its own movement toward completion. Adam contains the seeds of Christ, and Adam's anguish makes necessary and inevitable the sacrifice. In the same way the fragmented, alienated self seeks wholeness, which it may achieve after some symbolically self-destructive "rite of passage" (such as the "dark night of the soul," crucifixion, descent into Hades), from which it may emerge to new life.

This journey is the archetypal journey of the hero, and it is the journey of Lorca in *Poet in New York*. The poet calls for apocalypse for the modern civilization he sees in a state of morbid decay brought on by its loss of ritual. The apocalypse would serve as a symbolic ritual sacrifice, from which the society could be reborn. Correspondingly, the poet participates in the ritual by offering himself as the sacrificial lamb ("I offer myself to be eaten"), whereby he himself assumes the role of Christ. For by this symbolic self-destruction the poet reaches the climax of his anguish of separation and may thereafter move toward reconciliation with nature. The insatiable desire for a beyond recedes as the poet experiences a new wholeness in his identity with the force of the blood. And the poetry expressive of this wholeness assumes a more temporal form, finally falling into the incantatory rhythm (indicating a lower level of self-consciousness) of "Waltz in the branches" and "Sound of blacks in Cuba." The poetry approaches music, reproducing the rhythms of the universe.

# Notes

## Chapter 1

1. Lorca probably heard a talk at the Residencia de Estudiantes, where he lived, given by Louis Aragon on April 18, 1925, and later published in part under the title "Fragments d'une conférence" in the journal *La Révolution Surréaliste*, July 15, 1925. It was a condemnation of modern civilization in general: Aragon declared, "The age of metamorphosis is open. . . . Western world, you are condemned to death. . . . We will awaken everywhere the germs of confusion and malaise. We are the agitators of the spirit." (Angel Del Río, *Estudios sobre literatura contemporánea española* [Madrid: Gredos, 1966], pp. 284-85.)

2. Manuel Durán, "Introduction," in *Lorca*, ed. Manuel Durán (Englewood Cliffs, N.J.: Prentice-Hall, 1962), p. 1.

3. Marie Laffranque, *Les Idées esthétiques de Federico García Lorca* (Paris: Centre de Recherches Hispaniques, 1967), p. 165. Laffranque points out that many of the images of these poems resemble those which Dalí was employing at the time in his paintings: men reduced to the state of insects, giant ants, the throat pierced by a knife, and the self-mutilation of lovers.

4. Federico García Lorca, *Obras completas* (Madrid: Aguilar, 1969), p. 1654. This work is hereafter referred to in parentheses in the text.

## Chapter 2

1. See Federico García Lorca, *Obras completas*, pp. 211-12. In the poem "Cantos nuevos" ("New songs"), the poet cries out that he has a thirst for a song: "Song that may go to the soul of things/ and to the soul of the winds/ and that may finally rest in the bliss/ of the eternal heart."

2. The complete poem, translated, is as follows:

> The sea is
> the Lucifer of the blue.
> The sky fallen
> for wanting to be the light.
>
> Poor sea condemned               5
> to eternal movement,
> having before been
> quiet in the firmament!
>
> But from your bitterness
> love redeemed you.               10
> You gave birth to Venus pure,

and your depth remained
virgin and without pain.

Your sorrows are beautiful,
sea of glorious spasms.                                    15
But today instead of stars
you have green octopi.

Endure your suffering,
formidable Satan.
Christ walked on you,                                       20
but so did Pan.

The star Venus is
the harmony of the world.
May Ecclesiastes be quiet!
Venus is what is profound                                   25
in the soul . . .

. . . And miserable man
is a fallen angel.
Earth is the probable
Paradise lost.                                              30

3. Lorca, *Obras completas*, p. 268. In "Los álamos de plata" ("The poplars of silver"), written one month after "Mar," in May of 1919, Lorca says, "One must rest the body/ within the restless soul!/ One must blind his eyes with light from beyond!" The entire poem bears comparison with "Songs of the soul in rapture . . ." and "Other verses with a divine meaning by the same author," by Saint John of the Cross.

4. Edwin Honig, *García Lorca* (Norfolk, Conn.: New Directions, 1944), pp. 113-14.

5. See Denis de Rougemont, *Love in the Western World* (New York: Pantheon Books, 1956), p. 64. "Eros is complete Desire, luminous Aspiration, the primitive religious soaring carried to its loftiest pitch, to the extreme exigency of purity which is also the extreme exigency of Unity. But absolute unity must be the negation of the present human being in his suffering multiplicity. . . . [The demand of Eros] is to embrace no less than the All."

6. See Mircea Eliade, *The Sacred and the Profane*, trans. Willard R. Trask (New York: Harper and Brothers, 1961). Eliade says, "Revelation of a sacred space makes it possible to obtain a fixed point and hence to acquire orientation in the chaos of homogeneity. . . . The profane experience, on the contrary, maintains the homogeneity and hence the relativity of space. No true orientation is now possible, for the fixed point no longer enjoys a unique ontological status; it appears and disappears in accordance with the needs of the day" (pp. 23-24).

7. Ibid., p. 148.

8. See Carl G. Jung, *Modern Man in Search of a Soul*, trans. W. S. Dell and Cary F. Baynes (New York: Harcourt, Brace and World, 1933), p. 181, for a discussion of the Greek word *psyche*, which also means "butterfly."

9. J. E. Cirlot, *A Dictionary of Symbols*, trans. Jack Sage (New York: Philosophical Library, 1971), p. 65. I recognize that each poet will have his own symbolic system, which means that reference to such general studies as those by Cirlot, Jung, and Jacobi is inconclusive at best. Nonetheless, when used in

conjunction with an internal analysis of the whole of a poet's work, these studies may aid understanding.

10. Cecil Day-Lewis, *The Poetic Image* (New York: Oxford University Press, 1947), p. 50.

11. Susanne Langer, *Feeling and Form* (New York: Charles Scribner's Sons, 1953), pp. 236-37.

12. Angel Del Río, *Estudios sobre literatura contemporánea española* (Madrid: Gredos, 1966), p. 276.

13. Rollo May, "Psychology and the Daimonic," in *Myths, Dreams, and Religion*, ed. Joseph Campbell (New York: E. P. Dutton and Co., 1970), p. 209.

14. A possible connection may be made between the title of this poem and "Eden." Schonberg says that Lorca wrote these two poems during a summer stay at a beautiful lake in Vermont, of "virgin nature." See Jean-Louis Schonberg, *Federico García Lorca* (Mexico, D. F.: Compañía General de Ediciones, 1959), p. 236.

15. Cirlot, *A Dictionary of Symbols*, p. 152.

16. Carlos Bousoño, *Teoría de la expresión poética* (Madrid: Gredos, 1956), p. 76.

17. See Lorca, *Obras completas*, pp. 471, 476, and 491.

18. Perhaps this is an ironic parallel to the loaves and fishes with which Christ fed the multitudes.

19. See Alan Watts, *Myth and Ritual in Christianity* (Boston: Beacon Press, 1968), p. 160, for a discussion of the symbolism of the carpenter.

20. Joseph Frank, "Spatial Form in Modern Literature," *Sewanee Review* 53 (fall, 1945): 646-47.

## Chapter 3

1. Albert Camus, *The Myth of Sisyphus and Other Essays*, trans. Justin O'Brien (New York: Random House, 1955), p. 5.

2. J. E. Cirlot, *A Dictionary of Symbols*, trans. Jack Sage (New York: Philosophical Library, 1971), p. 65.

3. Jolande Jacobi, "Symbols in an Individual Analysis," in *Man and His Symbols*, ed. Carl G. Jung (Garden City, N.Y.: Doubleday and Co., 1972), p. 297.

4. Carl G. Jung, *Psyche and Symbol*, ed. Violet S. de Laszlo (New York: Doubleday and Co., 1958), pp. 127-28.

5. Rupert C. Allen, *The Symbolic World of Federico García Lorca* (Albuquerque: University of New Mexico Press, 1972), p. 17.

6. See Federico García Lorca, *Obras completas* (Madrid: Aguilar, 1969), p. 181: "All the roses are white, / as white as my sorrow."

7. Kenneth Burke, "The Poetic Process," in *Five Approaches of Literary Criticism*, ed. Wilbur S. Scott (New York: Collier Books, 1962), p. 75.

8. André Breton, *Manifestoes of Surrealism*, trans. Richard Seaver and Helen R. Lane (Ann Arbor: University of Michigan Press, 1969), p. 36.

9. See José Ortega y Gasset, *The Dehumanization of Art*, trans. Helen Weyl (Princeton: Princeton University Press, 1968).

## Chapter 4

1. Northrop Frye, *Fables of Identity: Studies in Poetic Mythology* (New York: Harcourt, Brace and World, Inc., 1963), p. 15.

2. Ibid. Frye says, "The pull of ritual is toward pure narrative."

3. See Susanne Langer, *Feeling and Form* (New York: Charles Scribner's Sons, 1953), pp. 351-66, for a discussion of tragedy as an enactment of the individual's predestined journey into death.

4. See Frye, *Fables of Identity*, pp. 19-20, for a catalogue of the "contents of the central pattern of the tragic and comic visions."

5. See Federico García Lorca, *Obras completas* (Madrid: Aguilar, 1969), p. 192. In this poem, "Mañana" ("Morning" or "Tomorrow"), the water of a natural fountain is the "blood of poets" flowing from the ground. In "New York: Office and denunciation," p. 515, the veins in a cat's paw are called "a world of broken rivers"; in that same poem Lorca identifies himself with the "river of young blood." In "Ode to Walt Whitman," p. 522, the American poet, the "Adam of blood," "dreamed of being a river," which means to flow with time.

6. Of Negroes, Lorca wrote: ". . . they are the most spiritual and most delicate of that world [of North America]. Because they believe, because they hope, because they sing and because they have an exquisite religious laziness that saves them from all their present dangerous jobs. . . . I wanted to write the poem of the Negro race in North America and emphasize the pain that the blacks suffer for being black in an adverse world; slaves of all the inventions of the white man and of all his machines, with the perpetual fear that they may forget one day to light the gas stove, or steer the automobile, or fasten the starched collar, or stick a fork in their eye. Because the inventions are not theirs. . . ."

7. Frye, *Fables of Identity*, pp. 19-20.

8. See Howard T. Young, *The Victorious Expression: A Study of Four Contemporary Poets* (Madison: The University of Wisconsin Press, 1966), p. 185. Young says, "Dammed-up blood becomes the symbol of blocked poetry."

9. See Rev. 8:7-8. This poem echoes the apocalyptic rhythm of destruction and resurrection in its structure, imagery, and theme, which pattern reappears in "Sleepless city."

10. The image of the desert suggests, as in *The Waste Land* and "The Hollow Men," the dryness of a spiritually empty world. It is land without a river—hence without physical or spiritual life.

11. In an effort to determine whether the word "hechos" was a misprint of the word "hecho," I checked translations by Ben Belitt and Stephen Spender and J. L. Gili. Ben Belitt interprets "hechos" to be a modifier of the implied "vosotros," in which case the poet is commanding the blacks to "be the humming pineapple" (my translation). See Federico García Lorca, *Poet in New York*, trans. Ben Belitt (New York: Grove Press, 1955), p. 25. Stephen Spender and J. L. Gili treat the line as if "hechos" were "hecho" (although in the Spanish version they use it is not) and thereby make the sun become the "buzzing cluster" (in their words). See Federico García Lorca, *The Selcted Poems of Federico García Lorca*, ed. Francisco García Lorca and Donald M. Allen (New York: New Directions Books, 1955), p. 121.

12. The Spanish word "piña" may mean either pineapple or pine cone. Although it is not evident from the context which meaning the poet had in mind, I have interpreted "piña" as pineapple, as have Spender and Gili, when it appears in line 21. Ben Belitt, on the other hand, interprets the word "piña" in line 21 as "peppery pine."

13. See Lorca, *Obras completas*, p. 281. In this poem, "Invocación al laurel" ("Invocation to the laurel," 1919), Lorca wrote, "Yo, como el barbudo mago de

los cuentos, sabía el lenguaje de flores y piedras" ("I, like the bearded magician of the stories, knew the language of flowers and stones").

14. The conquest of Wall Street by the jungle recalls the second stanza of "Christmas on the Hudson," p. 491, in which the primordial world of vegetation supplants the world of edges and angles. Here, in "Dance of death," the jungle–demonic opposite of the garden–represents the uncontrollable force of life which may be tragically destructive to man and his "frozen projects."

15. Perhaps the "fat woman" is a "Terrible Mother" image, signifying death, in which case she would symbolize spiritual death, or death-in-life. See J. E. Cirlot, *A Dictionary of Symbols*, trans. Jack Sage (New York: Philosophical Library, 1971), p. 218. Whether or not she would be defined as such by Jung, the "fat woman" would belong to the demonic world as described by Frye in *Fables of Identity*.

16. See Rupert C. Allen, *The Symbolic World of Federico García Lorca* (Albuquerque: University of New Mexico Press, 1972), pp. 17-18. Allen says, "The tambourine (like the drum) plays an important role in shamanistic rituals the world over as the means whereby the hypnotic trance is induced."

17. See Mircea Eliade, *The Two and the One*, trans. Willard R. Trask (New York: Harper and Brothers, 1961), p. 157. Eliade says, "As for men of traditional societies, the value they place on their food is part and parcel of their total behavior towards the Cosmos. By means of his food, man participates in a higher reality; he eats something that is rich, strong and confers prestige; which was created by the Supernatural Beings or even–in certain cases–is the substance of those Beings; which is, in any case, the product of a mystery. . . ."

18. Ibid., p. 158.

19. Langer, *Feeling and Form*, p. 351.

20. In the *Divine Comedy* the sin of excessive knowledge is represented by Ulysses, who reports that when his ship came into view of Mount Purgatory it was struck by a tempest and sunk; his sin is punishable in hell by God. By the twentieth century, however, with man's increased self-consciousness, the "sin" of excessive knowledge becomes its own punishment: vision becomes painful, paralyzing; it becomes hell itself. Tiresias, "throbbing between two lives," is modern man who has seen too much and now can "connect nothing with nothing." Jake Barnes is impotent. In Sartre's *Huis clos* the three sinners are tortured by the loss of their eyelids. The question is, "After such knowledge, what forgiveness?" (says Gerontion, "an old man in a dry month"). Will there by any salvation from the torment of unrelieved vision symbolized by sleeplessness in "Sleepless city"?

21. Rev. 9:4; 9:7.

22. Rev. 9:5-6.

23. Rev. 20:1.

24. From the Prayer for the Blessing of the Font, from the Liturgy of Holy Saturday in the *Roman Missal*, as quoted in Alan Watts, *Myth and Ritual in Christianity* (Boston: Beacon Press, 1968), pp. 46-47. Watts says, ". . . the 'heaven and earth' which God first created was a formless mass. Before he made anything else he made matter–*materia, matrix, mater*–as the maternal womb of the universe, for it is a general principle in mythology that material is the feminine component and spirit the masculine, their respective symbols being water or earth and air or fire. In the Christian myth every new creation is from water and the Spirit, for out of this conjunction the world is made, the Christ is born, and man is recreated through Baptism."

25. See Cirlot, *A Dictionary of Symbols*, pp. 222-23. Cirlot says, "Given the mystic and emanatistic character of the philosophy of symbolism whereby—as in Neoplatonism—the One is identified with the Creator, it follows that multiplicity must represent the farthest point from the Source of all things. If the image of the circle is taken to express the relationship between unity and multiplicity, then the centre corresponds to unity and the outer circumference or rim relates to multiplicity. . . . [M]ultiplicity, and its consequence, diversity, may be products of division as well as of multiplication. For symbolic purposes, the essence of multiplication is division. . . . Hence the negative character of multiplicity."

26. It has been noted that for Lorca there is a symbolic identification of river, blood, and poetry. Now all have been polluted by modern civilization. Accordingly, if the river retains its traditional symbolism as the individual life which flows into the sea of death (as in the "coplas" of Jorge Manrique), then it is the individual life that has been corrupted.

27. See Angel Del Río, *Estudios sobre literatura contemporánea española* (Madrid: Gredos, 1966), p. 281. Del Río notes the similarity between line 65 of this poem and the lines of Eliot's *The Waste Land*, "What shall I do now? What shall I do now? . . . Shall I at least set my lands in order?"

28. According to Del Río (in Lorca, *Poet in New York*, trans. Ben Belitt, p. xxv) "Sound of blacks in Cuba" was meant to be the last poem in the volume.

29. Igor Stravinsky, *Poetics of Music in the Form of Six Lessons*, trans. Arthur Knodel and Ingolf Dahl (Cambridge, Mass.: Harvard University Press, 1970), p. 97.

30. Richard Saez, "The Ritual Sacrifice in Lorca's *Poet in New York*," in *Lorca*, ed. Manuel Durán (Englewood Cliffs, N.J.: Prentice-Hall, 1962), pp. 108-29.

31. Saez refers to Del Río's observation of the similarity of Lorca's line 65 of "New York: Office and denunciation" and Eliot's "Shall I at least set my lands in order?" of *The Waste Land*.

# Bibliography

Allen, Rupert C. *The Symbolic World of Federico García Lorca*. Albuquerque: University of New Mexico Press, 1972.

Bousoño, Carlos. *Teoría de la expresión poética*. Madrid: Gredos, 1956.

Breton, André. *Manifestoes of Surrealism*. Translated by Richard Seaver and Helen R. Lane. Ann Arbor: University of Michigan Press, 1969.

———. *Le Surréalisme et la peinture*. Paris: Gallimard, 1965.

Burke, Kenneth. "The Poetic Process." In *Five Approaches of Literary Criticism*, edited by Wilbur S. Scott. New York: Collier Books, 1962.

Camus, Albert. *The Myth of Sisyphus and Other Essays*. Translated by Justin O'Brien. New York: Random House, 1955.

Cirlot, J. E. *A Dictionary of Symbols*. Translated by Jack Sage. New York: Philosophical Library, 1971.

Day-Lewis, Cecil. *The Poetic Image*. London: Oxford University Press, 1947.

Del Río, Angel. *Estudios sobre literatura contemporánea española*. Madrid: Gredos, 1966.

Durán, Manuel. Introduction to *Lorca: A Collection of Critical Essays*. Twentieth Century Views, edited by Manuel Durán. Englewood Cliffs, N.J.: Prentice-Hall, 1962.

Eliade, Mircea. *The Sacred and the Profane*. Translated by Willard R. Trask. New York: Harper and Brothers, 1961.

———. *The Two and the One*. Translated by J. M. Cohen. New York: Harper and Row, 1962.

Frank, Joseph. "Spatial Form in Modern Literature." *Sewanee Review* 53, nos. 2 and 4 (spring, fall, 1945): 221-40, 643-53.

Frye, Northrop. *Fables of Identity: Studies in Poetic Mythology*. New York: Harcourt, Brace and World, 1963.

García Lorca, Federico. *Obras completas*. 15th ed. Madrid: Aguilar, 1969.

———. *Poet in New York*. Translated by Ben Belitt. New York: Grove Press, 1955.

García Lorca, Federico. *The Selected Poems of Federico García Lorca.* Edited by Francisco García Lorca and Donald M. Allen. New York: New Directions Books, 1955.

Honig, Edwin. *García Lorca.* Norfolk, Conn.: New Directions, 1944.

Jacobi, Jolande. "Symbols in an Individual Analysis." In *Man and His Symbols,* edited by Carl G. Jung. Garden City, N.Y.: Doubleday and Company, 1972.

Jung, Carl G. *Modern Man in Search of a Soul.* Translated by W. S. Dell and Cary F. Baynes. New York: Harcourt, Brace and World, 1933.

————. *The Portable Jung.* Edited by Joseph Campbell; translated by R. F. C. Hull. New York: The Viking Press, 1971.

————. *Psyche and Symbol.* Edited and translated by Violet S. Laszlo. New York: Doubleday and Company, 1958.

Laffranque, Marie. *Les Idées esthétiques de Federico García Lorca.* Paris: Centre de Recherches Hispaniques, 1967.

Langer, Susanne K. *Feeling and Form.* New York: Charles Scribner's Sons, 1953.

May, Rollo. "Psychotherapy and the Daimonic." In *Myths, Dreams, and Religion,* edited by Joseph Campbell. New York: E. P. Dutton and Company, 1970.

Ortega y Gasset, José. *The Dehumanization of Art.* Translated by Helen Weyl. Princeton: Princeton University Press, 1968.

Rougemont, Denis de. *Love in the Western World.* New York: Pantheon Books, 1956.

Saez, Richard. "The Ritual Sacrifice in *Lorca's Poet in New York.*" In *Lorca: A Collection of Critical Essays.* Twentieth Century Views, edited by Manuel Durán. Englewood Cliffs, N.J.: Prentice-Hall, 1962.

Schonberg, Jean-Louis. *Federico García Lorca.* Mexico, D.F.: Compañía General de Ediciones, S.A., 1959.

Stravinsky, Igor. *Poetics of Music in the Form of Six Lessons.* Translated by Arthur Knodel and Ingolf Dahl. Cambridge, Mass.: Harvard University Press, 1970.

Watts, Alan W. *Myth and Ritual in Christianity.* Boston: Beacon Press, 1968.

Young, Howard T. *The Victorious Expression: A Study of Four Contemporary Spanish Poets.* Madison: University of Wisconsin Press, 1966.

# Index